Revive, Refresh, Renew

30 DAYS OF PRAYER & DEVOTION

CRYSTAL LOVE

EDITED BY
NICOLE QUEEN

VISION PUBLISHING
HOUSE

Copyright © 2022 by Crystal Love

All rights reserved.

No part of this book may be reproduced in any form or by any electronic or mechanical means, including information storage and retrieval systems, without written permission from the author, except for the use of brief quotations in a book review.

ISBN: 978-1-7353377-2-2 (Paperback)

Vision Publishing House
9103 Woodmore Centre #334
Lanham, MD 20706

www.vision-publishinghouse.com

Contents

Introduction	v
Day 1	1
Day 2	9
Day 3	17
Day 4	23
Day 5	27
Day 6	33
Day 7	39
Day 8	45
Day 9	51
Day 10	55
Day 11	59
Day 12	65
Day 13	71
Day 14	75
Day 15	81
Day 16	87
Day 17	93
Day 18	97
Day 19	103
Day 20	109
Day 21	115
Day 22	121
Day 23	127
Day 24	133
Day 25	139
Day 26	145
Day 27	151
Day 28	155
Day 29	159
Day 30	165
Bonus: Day 31	171
Bonus: Day 32	175

Affirmations	179
Promises of God	181
Daily Prayer	187
Final Message	191
About the Author	193

Introduction

Are you ready for a change? In the next thirty days, this book will ignite your flame and motivate you to return or approach a new life of consistent prayer, while sparking a challenge in you to be bold and intentional about your future.

It's time to reignite your flame. Has your flame gone out? Let's take a thirty-day journey of dedication to blazing a trail into God's presence. Let God lead the way! If it's a trail, this means you're not the only one who will benefit, but others will follow. We are coming home on the pathway of our Father.

This devotional is also for those who haven't had the drive to live, dream, and stay motivated to accomplish God's plan for their life. We all reach crossroads in our lives where it seems as if what we were doing isn't working anymore. When things get that way, it's time to be *revived*, *refreshed*, and *renewed*.

Let's be intentional about our forward progression in life and make everyday strides to produce what we were created to do. It's not about how fast you move; it's about your progression. So, prepare your life to be changed— one step at a time.

INTRODUCTION

This book includes devotionals, Scriptures, and prayers for daily use! Also included are prayers and instrumental worship digital downloads to guide you along your journey. It is my prayer that God touches your heart and mind each day, enabling you to see the beauty of His love for you and how special you are in His sight!

Scan below to access your digital resources.

Password: Listen

Day 1
RISE & SHINE

I*t's time to rise and shine.*
Life experiences may cause you to be in a low place from time to time. And when you feel low, you may take a moment and think to yourself: *Is there any hope for me, and will I ever get out of this place? Why is it so hard to rise and stay there, at least for a little while?*

I have always been fascinated with how the mind works, and how it relates to us as humans when it comes to our reactions regarding how we respond to life. As far as I can remember, I have had a negative mindset regarding many aspects, and I couldn't understand why until I reached adulthood. There would be certain occurrences that would happen that would cause me to go into a low place. *What is a low place?* When certain memories would come to mind from certain events in life that weren't so pleasurable, almost instantly, my whole mood would change. This negative response to a familiar action led to these three steps:

1. I would leave wherever I was at the moment. And if I couldn't leave, I would socially and mentally shut down. So, though I was physically there, I checked out until I could physically leave.
2. I would go home, turn the lights out, and lie in bed for as long as I could.

3. I would shut everyone out—no calls, no food, no TV, etc. Everything from the outside world would be shut off because I didn't want anyone to see me in this place.

It didn't matter what the situation was; it could have been a new occurrence or something that reminded me of a past event. I always went back to this *familiar* place; it was my safe place. No one would bother me here. I didn't have to be questioned about how I feel and why I would continue this vicious cycle of self-inflicted hurt. I allowed depression to grip me every time something negative—whether physical or in my thoughts—caused me to react this way. It was familiar, and it was my safe place. I programmed my mind to react this way all the time.

There were times when I decided to get help because I knew this was unhealthy, and it would lead to other destructive avenues to relieve the pain. Familiarity is one of the reasons why it may be difficult to always resort to a low place when difficulties in life occur.

One of the definitions of *familiarity* according to the Merriam-Webster Dictionary is "a state of close relationship." Something about this situation triggered one of the same emotions from a previous event and caused you to react the same way as before. You resort to this mindset and react similarly in your physical state because it is comfortable, and your mind has been programmed to respond this way. The power of one thought can change the course of your entire moment, day, week, month, year, and life.

In order to rise above this way of thinking, you need to create new thoughts. This reminds me of the Scripture from Philippians 4:7, "And the peace of God, which passeth all understanding, shall keep your hearts and minds through Christ Jesus."

Peace is the first step to having a clear mind. *Peace* according to Merriam-Webster Dictionary is "freedom from disquieting or oppressive thoughts or emotions." Even here, the definition of *peace* relates to the thoughts in your mind and emotions. So, we have to be free from our own mind.

Thoughts are created from life experiences. These are recorded and called memories, which are filtered through your conscious and subconscious. This is why our mind has to be free. The Scripture says in Romans 12:2, "Do not be conformed to this world, but be transformed by the renewing of your mind. Then you will be able to test and approve what God's will is— His good, pleasing, and perfect will."

The truth of the Word of God will give us freedom in all areas. The peace of God can never be measured or limited. You can choose to rest in it, daily. *How do you do this?* You do this by allowing the spirit of freedom to become your way of living through washing daily in the Word of God.

That he might sanctify and cleanse it with the washing of water by the word.

— EPHESIANS 5:26

Being not conformed to the world is a daily practice and can only be done by the help of the Lord and dying to your flesh with much discipline. We cannot live this life in our own strength. Negative or positive thoughts will always crowd your mind. You have to allow God to filter those thoughts. The world feeds the problem with more negativity instead of releasing it to the Lord in the prayer of supplication. When problems come and trigger an emotion, cast your cares upon the Lord (1 Peter 5:7) before you react. Embrace the peace, and react in your liberated place.

Reprogram - revise or rewrite a program
Program – planned series of future events
(*Merriam-Webster Dictionary*)

In order to reprogram something, you have to know what you want to replace the information with. This is why the Scripture says old things are passed away, and behold, all things become new (2 Corinthians 5:17). We have to press delete and add what we want to see. So, this goes to show you that our memories have control. They are scheduled programs in our minds that we replay over and over again. We relive the whole event and how they made us feel, and we confirm future actions to those past emotions.

It's time to rewrite your story and make new memories. Everything about your life moving forward should be new.

So, you then write down what you want your life to be moving forward. God has surely given you glimpses of what He wants for you. *How do you work on those things? What do you do to create these new memories?* Start with one thing at a time. Have daily affirmations! Pray and ask God how to start your new life and what to do to accomplish the new tasks. He has the manual regarding how to live this new life.

> *Memories* – the power or process of reproducing or recalling what has been learned and retained
> (*Merriam-Webster Dictionary*)

Just imagine if our mind is in good standing, how powerful we could be at reproducing and following through on the positive to execute, remembering the negative, and learning from its consequences, so that we won't follow through and react on old memories. As we go through life, we remember what happens, add to that development in a specific area, and grow. Stored-up memories—both bad and good—get you through school, from Kindergarten to High School. They help you get through life, as well. You can allow it to either impact you and move forward or suppress you and stay stuck.

> *Father God, in the Name of Jesus, I present my mind to you today. I realize that I don't have the ability within myself to change and reprogram my mind. But You said in Your Word that if I keep my mind stayed on You, then You will keep me in perfect peace (Isaiah 26:3) and to be transformed by the renewing of my mind (Romans 12:2). So, I present my body today, a living sacrifice holy and acceptable, which is my reasonable service (Romans 12:1). I surrender all to You, and I know that through the Word of God, my thinking will change. I will be washed daily with the Word (Ephesians 5:26). I will see evidence of the*

transforming of my mind and actions in Jesus' Name. Amen.

* * *

Take a moment to think, reflect, pray, and meditate. As you are praying, God will begin to highlight what to write regarding what's needed in your life to move forward according to His will.

Reflect/Journal

Day 2
MIND THE MATTER

The human mind is 10% conscious, 50–60% subconscious, and 30–40% unconscious (Dr. C. Demarco).

Why am I honing in on the mind? The mind is the battleground that filters out what you will respond to. I want to state a few scientific facts about the mind.

The conscious mind is the captain of the ship. It communicates to the outside world and inner self through speech, pictures, writing, physical movement, and thought.

The subconscious mind is in charge of our recent memories and is in continuous contact with the resources of the unconscious mind. These memories are closer to the surface and more easily accessible with a little focus.

The unconscious mind constantly communicates with the conscious via subconscious and is what provides us with the meaning to all our interactions with the world, as filtered through our beliefs and habits. It communicates through feelings, emotions, imagination, sensations, and dreams. It is a storage place for all our memories that have been repressed or those that we don't wish to recall. We can't pull out this memory at our choosing. We can't remember without some special technique or event. Memories stored since birth form and reinforce your beliefs, habits, and behaviors over time.

Your subconscious is the storage place of all your memories, emotions, and habits. And in fact, it is very good at reasoning and logic. If all you do is focus your conscious thoughts continually on negative things, then your subconscious will obediently deliver the feelings, emotions, and memories that you associated with that type of thinking. Because those feelings will become a reality, you can then be caught up in a never-ending loop of negativity, fear, and anxiety, constantly looking for the bad in every situation. Our mental thoughts are probably the only one true freedom we have in this world that we can actually control. The work desk of the mind is the subconscious mind.

After discussing the details about the mind and how God made and formed things to be, it makes sense why God said in His Word that we have to be born again, transformed, and given a new heart and right spirit. We were born in sin and shaped in iniquity. All of the good that was imparted from the foundation of the world was seared by sin. Sin kills the good and doesn't allow us to see the light. So we were sin-conscious before we were God-conscious when born into the world. This is why we have to be born again in the spirit, and our soul has to be saved from the damage of sin. We have to be renewed, reprogrammed, and reconciled with our Father. Sin didn't allow us to know we had a choice to be free. When we get saved, we begin to grow in God. It seems so right, like it's something we should have been doing all along. The closer we get to God, the more aware we become of who we are and what we were originally designed for. It's such a fight because sin is a natural first-known response to our mental and spiritual state of being.

Before I knew the effects or functions of the conscious, unconscious, and subconscious, I would pray that my subconscious to be filtered out. I did not like it when my conscious mind would react to my subconscious. When you allow people or things to control you that are not actively in your life, you are being held captive to a memory that will keep playing as long as you allow the rewind button to keep playing it back and reliving it all over again. It's easy to say you're going to move forward in life one day, and the next day something triggers your thought pattern. You say to yourself, "I felt so good. I felt like I was rising above it, and now I'm back to ground zero." Instead of immediately soaring above the power of that thought or occurrence, you feel so bad that you allowed it to get you back to that place that you decide to stay there.

I know that someone out there is reading this, saying to themselves, "Wow, this is me! How can I stop this?"

This book may not be for everyone, but I went through different things in life, and I made it through to share and help someone else. It was all worth it because you're reading this, and you will be *free* when you're done! I'm sure of it!

The Bible says in John 8:36, "If the Son sets you free, you will be free indeed." Now, I won't assume that everyone reading this book has every read the Bible and know who the "Son" is and how freedom comes from someone I haven't formally introduced you to. Well, you are now introduced to the Son, whose name is Jesus; His Father is named God.

There are many beliefs out here in the world, as well as, many gods that people choose to worship. However, there is only one true and living God that should be worshipped, and He created the entire universe and everything in it. I was taught as a little girl that God was real and that because sin or evil existed in the world, God sent his son Jesus to die as a sacrifice for the sins of this world, so that we can be free from sin and not become a slave to it.

The steps to being saved from sin and the effects of it are simply these:

1. Repent of all your sins.
2. Acknowledge that God's son Jesus died for our sins and redeemed us back to God because we were separated from God because of sin.
3. Find a Bible-teaching church and live out this life every day with God's leading.

We all have a purpose in life. When God handmade us all individually, it was with a purpose in mind. We can only find out what that is by praying and asking God to show us. If we can take a moment just to think about the things that we enjoy doing or have imagined ourselves doing in life, usually in those things and thoughts, we can sometimes find bits and pieces to this puzzle called life. Along the way, we find that it's more than one thing we may have a passion, ability, or love for. We have to pray and ask God what and how to get those things going in life.

The way God made us, with regards to how our mind operates, is our protection. If we remembered and reacted to everything that happened (every emotion that we react to is based on present or past circumstances), we would be imbalanced.

There are many people in the world who have lost total use of their mind because they don't have divine help to give them healing from the negative things that happen. In most people's minds, this makes someone crazy, as some people may classify it.

> *In the same way, let your light shine before others, that they may see your good deeds and glorify your Father in heaven.*
>
> *— MATTHEW 5:16*

> *The light shines in the darkness, and the darkness has not overcome it.*
>
> *— JOHN 1:5*

> *Father, in the Name of Jesus, I pray that I be renewed in the faculties of my mind. Though my mind can appear to be complicated in the natural sense, today, I choose to walk in the spirit. I declare that I will live in the spirit. I declare that all past thoughts and difficulties will be my testimony of Your redemption and healing. I arm myself today with the helmet of salvation guarding my head and protecting me from the blows of doubt from the enemy.*
>
> *Father, I thank You for I am protected and not exposed on the spiritual battlefield. I put on salvation today and every day that my entire person will walk on wholeness. In Jesus' Name. Amen.*

* * *

Take a moment to think, reflect, pray, and meditate. As you are praying, God will begin to highlight what to write regarding what's needed in your life to move forward according to His will.

Reflect/Journal

Day 3
TAKE THE POSITIVE OUT OF THE NEGATIVE

Just like the positive and negative ends of a battery have to connect in order to work, we have to pull out the positive from the negative experiences as lessons learned. Sometimes, it's a process that has to be walked and talked through, daily. I think the most difficult part about this is that we may try to drown out the negative like it did not happen and convince ourselves that it no longer affects us. If we were really honest with ourselves, the process of healing and moving forward would be more progressive and effective— if we embraced our current season. Once we do that, we can enter into the next one.

Moving on and forward is a choice. Some people may blame situations and others for the reason why things happen in their lives. However, some things happen as a byproduct, and others, we have no control over. Regardless of circumstance, we still have a say regarding how we respond to life's circumstances.

Our errors in life shape our character, all the way from childhood to adulthood. When we first touched the stove and it was hot, we knew because of the pain of the burn and that permanent scar, that we should no longer get close to the stove because we want to avoid the pain. Even after learning this aspect, I've still burned myself, after knowing the stove (or oven) was hot, despite touching it by mistake. So, even when we try to avoid things, we are still confronted with them, and eventually, we have to deal with them over time. Some roads just have to be traveled, as it is a part of life.

We have to look at the story of Jesus and how His life was necessary, even though it was filled with so many obscurities that would have caused anyone to doubt their faith and question God— which, in fact, Jesus, the Savior of the world, did Himself. It will all serve a purpose. All the pain and joys mixed together make our lives a beautiful painting mixed with the colors of life. Sometimes, we need additional help— someone who we are accountable to for our actions. It could be a counselor, good friend with sound advice, or your pastor— someone who will help you in this journey to wholeness.

> *And he has identified us as his own by placing the Holy Spirit in our hearts as the first installment that guarantees everything he has promised us.*
>
> — 2 CORINTHIANS 1:22

> *But thank God! He has made us his captives and continues to lead us along in Christ's triumphal procession. Now he uses us to spread the knowledge of Christ everywhere, like a sweet perfume.*
>
> — 2 CORINTHIANS 2:14–15

Our lives are a Christlike fragrance rising up to God.

> *Father God, I pray that my life will produce the fragrance that reaches up to You and spread to everyone that I come in contact with. I thank You for the Holy Spirit that You have given as an installment that guarantees everything that You promised. I thank You that I am no longer held captive by the discrepancies in my own heart. I am captivated by the infinite love that*

You have for me. You have shown this love by rescuing me from the destruction of my identity that was caused by sin that was in me and a part of my nature. Because of Your sacrifice, I am able to walk in the light of Your Word and be directed by the revelation of what my life should look like. I pray that the more I learn of You, abide in You, and rely on you, the more I will know who I am and carry out my purpose in the earth. Thank You for the victory in my life today and the rest of the days of my life. In Jesus' Name. Amen.

Take a moment to think, reflect, pray, and meditate. As you are praying, God will begin to highlight what to write regarding what's needed in your life to move forward according to His will.

CRYSTAL LOVE

Reflect/Journal

Day 4
BALANCE YOUR EXPECTATIONS

What is balance and expectation? *Balance*, according to Merriam-Webster Dictionary, is "mental and emotional steadiness." This is a conscious decision, every day, to move in balance. Let the balance in your mind level out. It's okay for something to bother you, sometimes. If that happens, how you respond to it is key, and how you let your feelings about it linger on is important. We cannot allow ourselves to be numb to human emotions. That isn't the thing that becomes the problem; it's how we handle our emotions.

The Bible has a Scripture from Ezekiel 36:26 where it talks about the new heart that God will give us. All through life, our heart has been filled with emotions, both painful and joyful. What's in our heart connects with our mind. These two compartments are partners that work together and make us who we are. When these two are not partnered, filtered, and balanced, we will hit many pitfalls, train wrecks, and disasters in life that take so long to recover from and repair. This is so discouraging when you feel that you haven't made progress in life, and you keep repeating cycles. We have to make a conscious effort and ask God to repair both; this will help create and keep balance.

> *I will give you a new heart and put a new spirit in you; I*
> *will remove from you your heart of stone and give you*
> *a heart of flesh. And I will put my Spirit in you and*

> *move you to follow my decrees and be careful to keep my laws.*
>
> — EZEKIEL 36:26–27

Father God, You are the scale from which everything in my life is balanced. When I'm off balance from one extreme to the next, I pray that you always bring me back to You, the center of life. The core of who I am is in You. Today, the focus of life centers on Your plan and Your purpose for me. I pray that today, there will be a realignment of my heart, mind, and spirit, so that You will reach the core of me. Who I am and who I am to become is who You created me to be. Let today mark the beginning of balance— a balance in time, as it pertains to family, prayer, career, love, functionality, creativity, and every area of importance that God highlights to me.

As I pray, I am open to Your instruction and guidance to bring order and balance to my life, to lead me toward the path in You that I was predestined to take. Thank You for being a lamp unto my feet and a light unto my path. In Jesus' Name. Amen.

* * *

Take a moment to think, reflect, pray, and meditate. As you are praying, God will begin to highlight what to write regarding what's needed in your life to move forward according to His will.

REVIVE, REFRESH, RENEW

Reflect/Journal

Day 5

GROW ME UP (SPIRITUAL GROWTH)

What do you think of when you hear the term *spiritual growth*? *Spiritual* means connecting with the one and only, true and living God. In order for something to grow, it has to first be planted. Is the soil of your spirit broken up? Are you ready to plant?

The soil has to be tested to determine where it's compacted or poorly drained. The area has to be free of chemical spills or anything hazardous to its growth. Take careful examination of your motives.

Do we want to be close to God for materialistic things, or do we want to know His heart so that we can complete His agenda here on earth? What are we planting that we want to grow? What do you feel, today, that you need more of spiritually to connect to God? You need to be planted in love and prayer, study the Bible, and connect with other spiritually grounded people.

Name at least three things that will help you grow in this season of your life. Take a moment, meditate, and pray. As you begin to journal today, the Holy Spirit will reveal what needs to be done in this season of your life.

Discipline and consistency are the key to growing. You have to feed the need. Spiritual food is needed for spiritual growth. A farmer knows what to do when it comes to the seeds that he has planted because he has done his research and studied the seasons, soil, seed, and harvest.

Growing doesn't happen on its own. God has put everything in place that we need for the earth to produce— soil for the ground, seeds from the trees, food from the ground, and rain from the sky.

Planting has to be done first, and the Word of God does the watering. How hungry are you? Will you dedicate every day to watering and be washed in the Word of God?

> *Make her holy, cleansing her by the washing with water through the word.*
>
> — EPHESIANS 5:26

> *I have planted, Apollos watered; but God gave the increase.*
>
> — 1 CORINTHIANS 3:6

> *The earth is the LORD'S, and the fullness thereof; the world, and they that dwell therein.*
>
> — PSALM 24:1

> *Now no shrub had yet appeared on the earth and no plant had yet sprung up, for the LORD God had not sent rain on the earth and there was no one to work the ground, but streams came up from the earth and watered the whole surface of the ground. Then the LORD God formed a man from the dust of the ground and breathed into his nostrils the breath of life, and the man became a living being. Now the LORD God had planted a garden in the east, in Eden; and there he put the man he had formed. The LORD God made all kinds of trees grow out of the ground-trees that were pleasing to the eye and good for food. In the middle of the garden were the tree of life and the tree of the knowledge of good and evil.*
>
> — GENESIS 2:5–9

In the beginning God created the heavens and the earth.

— GENESIS 1:1

The LORD is close to the brokenhearted and saves those who are crushed in spirit.

— PSALM 34:18

God, My Father, my devotion today is to You. My dependence is on You. My hope and trust are in You. I believe that Your promises will be made manifest in my life. I believe that there will be a consistent flow of the manifestation of who You have created me to be in the earth because I have devoted my life to You. I am liberated in knowing of Your way and knowing that it's perfect. I don't have to strive to be something that You already imparted in me through the working of the Holy Spirit.

When you sent Your son Jesus to die on the Cross for my sins, righteousness and redemption were applied. So, I will rest in You and let You do Your perfect will in me. I pray that I will continue to allow the Word of God to wash me and illuminate my senses, so that what is done in my body will glorify You. I wash my hands of the past works done in hopes to gain what You have freely given through that work of the Cross.

Today, I receive my benefits. The righteousness of God has imputed my debt as paid in full, and has given me the priestly robe of royalty to walk and live life in the authority and power of the Holy Spirit. I am no longer a slave to my old nature. I am a new creature in God.

> *God, water my garden so that I can and produce the seeds and experience supernatural growth that will grow and expand beyond myself. My prayer is that I won't stray from Your commandments and that I stay connected to the vine. I will continue to produce the fruit in its due season and reap the harvest, in Jesus' Name. Amen.*

* * *

Take a moment to think, reflect, pray, and meditate. As you are praying, God will begin to highlight what to write regarding what's needed in your life to move forward according to His will.

Reflect/Journal

Day 6
EXPECTATIONS IN PERSPECTIVE

Expectation means "to be certain or look forward to," according to Merriam-Webster Dictionary. Philippians 4:6–7 says, "Don't fret or worry. Instead of worrying, pray." Let petitions and praises shape your worries into prayers. Put expectations in perspective. We can expect God to do exceedingly and abundantly above all that we ask or think, according to the power that works in us. We have to set expectations, or else we will never have the mindset that it will ever happen for us. We can put a demand on people to expect them to do things, and this can disappoint us to the point where it will destroy relationships and self-worth, if you depend on people to be the pentacle from which your esteem is built. When we understand that when the Bible says not to put your trust in man because they will surely let you down, this should help us guard some of our disappointments when it comes to relationships. Psalms 118:8 says, "It is better to take refuge in the Lord than to trust in humans." The human ability is limited without God's wisdom and guidance.

Life, sometimes, can leave you so full of hurt and pain, as well as disappointments and expectations from those who are dear to you. You have to try to deal with life from God's perspective. If not, you may struggle with wanting to live, thinking that life is unfair and that you aren't loved. Love can cause you to experience hurt. Love is what makes you care enough to hurt when someone has treated you unfairly. Release it to God, forgive, love your enemies, and then pray for those who despitefully use you. We can expect God to do what He promised because His Word is true.

In Hebrews 6:13–14, for example, there was God's promise to Abraham. Since there was no one greater to swear by, God took an oath in His own Name, saying, "I will certainly bless you, and I will multiply your descendants beyond number." Now this is something to stand on, and God wants to make it very clear that we can put expectations on anything that will line up with His Word. It will surely happen, so expect it.

> *For all of God's promises find their "yes" of fulfillment in him. And as his "yes" and our "amen" ascend to God, we bring him glory.*
>
> *— 2 CORINTHIANS 1:20–22*

> *It is better to take refuge in the Lord than to trust in man.*
>
> *— PSALM 118:8*

> *My Father, my Savior, my Love, I am relieved that I can take refuge in You. You are my safe place, my Way out and in, and my Defender. I can depend on You for safety and provision. I know that You are not like man and can never be compared to anyone in the earth. So, I look to You who is the author and the perfecter of my faith (Hebrews 12:2). You have started and finished the story of my life, and I have the faith to trust Your finished work. And because You started it, I know You will finish it. You're working through me; everything that You do is good (Psalm 26:3). Because You said that goodness and mercy shall follow me all the days of my life, I will trust You every day, as it yields the fruit that it's supposed to bear. As I draw nigh to You, and my faith increases by hearing the Word of God, allow my dependence on man to*

lessen, as my reliability on You increases (Romans 10:17). I expect an enhanced version of me to manifest, because through You, my imperfections will serve a greater glory that's being produced through my trials and tests. In Jesus' Name. Amen.

* * *

Take a moment to think, reflect, pray, and meditate. As you are praying, God will begin to highlight what to write regarding what's needed in your life to move forward according to His will.

Reflect/Journal

Day 7

THE IMPORTANCE OF CONSISTENCY

Many of us may wake up one day and say, "Hey, I want to start a business. I have a creative idea that I would like to get off the ground." You may do the basic footwork of that particular thing, and be so enthused and motivated. We may even share it with a friend, mentor, pastor, etc. Some people may volunteer to help. You may plan an event, and it may even be a great success! But the problem is, do we bask in the success of a great start? Or, do you forget to plan to move on to the next thing?

Consistency means that you're able to keep whatever you are doing at a stable pace, to its best potential. Do you have the ability to do the same thing over and over again, at a steady pace, to see progression? Always add to what you're doing and do not take away. You can regroup and revamp, but be consistent and determined to keep moving forward. Make a vow to yourself to finish strong. You're going on a path where you may experience some hills, inclines, valleys, muddy areas, rain, hail, sleet, and snow, but will you remain consistent? Pray, plan, and execute! You will never know what the end will be, or the potential of what you are doing, if you do not remain consistent, pouring in the same or even more energy to keep it going. If you keep going, you will see results!

As for us, we have all of these great witnesses who encircle

> *us like clouds. So, we must let go of every wound that has pierced us and the sin we so easily fall into. Then we will be able to run life's marathon race with passion and determination for the path has been already marked out for us.*
>
> — HEBREWS 12:1-2

We must look away from the natural realm, and fasten our gaze onto Jesus, who birthed faith within us and Who leads us forward into faith's perfection.

> *My Beloved, I have never found anyone to be as faithful as You. I wake up every day in receipt of Your grace and mercy. I am grateful to see the promises of God manifested today. This is the day where something is awakened that I never knew existed. Lord, awaken the fire in me that I may run with vigor. Deepen my roots in You, as I spend time saturated in communion with You— being captivated by Your Words, arming myself for the battle that You have already won, and embracing my victory. I have won because You have won; the Father has won. Draw me closer to You, God, until You and I are one.*

Declaration of Scripture:
Joined Together in Perfect Unity

> *Look at how much encouragement you've found in your relationship with the Anointed One! You are filled to overflowing with his comforting love. You have experienced a deepening friendship with the Holy Spirit and have felt his tender affection and mercy. So I'm asking you, my friends, that you be joined together*

> *in perfect unity—with one heart, one passion, and united in one love. Walk together with one harmonious purpose and you will fill my heart with unbounded joy.*
> *Be free from pride-filled opinions, for they will only harm your cherished unity. Don't allow self-promotion to hide in your hearts, but in authentic humility put others first and view others as more important than yourselves.*
> *Abandon every display of selfishness. Possess a greater concern for what matters to others instead of your own interests.*
> *And consider the example that Jesus, the Anointed One, has set before us. Let his mindset become your motivation.*
>
> — PHILIPPIANS 2:1–5

. . .

Some may ask why you have to arm yourself for a battle that has already been won, thinking that you don't have to fight. The fight is in the mind. We must arm ourselves with the Word of God, so that we can win every spiritual battle that is set before us. We must walk through it to our victory to obtain it, from one destination to the next, so that others may see that we are running too, and be encouraged. We are covering territory, claiming what's already ours. We are casting down every imagination that exalts itself against the knowledge of God.

Your thoughts control your actions. What you believe will determine what you conceive. What you conceive will grow. This conception by supernatural divine impartation will produce nothing but exponential results.

Song of Declaration (Listen To):
"You Won't Relent" by Misty Edwards

> "Come be the fire inside of me. Come be the flame upon my heart, until you and I are one!"

* * *

Take a moment to think, reflect, pray, and meditate. As you are praying, God will begin to highlight what to write regarding what's needed in your life to move forward according to His will.

REVIVE, REFRESH, RENEW

Reflect/Journal

Day 8
REMAIN PRAYERFUL

Prayer gives us that positive affirmation because we are communicating with our power source. What is your foundation? Prayer will help us remain devoted and remain consistent. Wouldn't it be amazing if we can decide to devote time and be consistent in our prayer life? How effective would our lives be if we really consulted God regarding how and when to move forward, what to do, and when to do it? Just imagine how much would be accomplished if we communicated with our creator on a daily basis. This will save time and increase our progress.

God wants us to follow every step and instruction to live a productive life. Every moment communicating with our Savior and spending time with Him are moments worth having. Minutes in prayer can save us from pitfalls, prepare us for any situation that we face, and give us peace while experiencing chaos all around us. Time in prayer can give you direction for your entire life. God doesn't give us everything at once, as there is a season for everything. So, He will only release things based upon what we can handle at the time.

Prayers are not just about receiving information, but they're about falling in love with our Father in heaven, receiving His love, so that we can pour it out on others. I challenge you to keep a prayer journal and track what you pray for. Now, understand that we seek God for relationship, not blessings. He promises that He will never leave us, and He supplies all of our needs according to His riches in glory; these promises are true and final. Prayer opens the door of intimacy with God; therefore, it shows you who you are, revealing your identity. How would you know the essence of what's inside of you if you did not meet and become well-acquainted with the One who created you? Get to know God, and as He shows you Himself, you will learn more of who you are and are becoming.

> *Be joyful in hope, patient in affliction, persistent in prayer.*
>
> — ROMANS 12:12

> *Father God, I thank You for the opportunity to pray, to come boldly to the throne of grace with no middle man (Hebrews 4:16). I humble myself under Your mighty Hand and commit myself to communion with You with, daily (1 Peter 5:6). For You are the source of my strength and my daily bread (Matthew 6:11). Today will mark the day that my flame will be ignited to stay consistent in prayer (Colossians 4:12), praying in the spirit Your will in the earth (Ephesians 6:18). Thy Kingdom come and Thy Will be done on earth, as it is in heaven (Matthew 6:10). I pray that my heart will be in alignment with Your heart, as I know that my ways and thoughts are unlike Yours.*
>
> *Father, may I become one with You and in perfect harmony with the forward progression of Your plan in the earth. My life is in Your hands. You are in control. Use me as a vessel of clay on the Potter's wheel, molded (Jeremiah 18:4) into who You have designed*

for me to be from the foundation of the world (Jeremiah 1:5). In Jesus' Name. Amen.

* * *

Take a moment to think, reflect, pray, and meditate. As you are praying, God will begin to highlight what to write regarding what's needed in your life to move forward according to His will.

Reflect/Journal

Day 9

SOARING IN TURBULENCE

Imagine yourself on a plane traveling to your destination. The pilot tells everyone to buckle their seat belts and prepare for takeoff. You have one thing in mind: getting to your destination. In your mind, you want to make it safely to your destination.

The plane has taken off smoothly, and you are high in the air. You can no longer see the ground beneath you—no people, trees, buildings, or noise. When you look out of the window, you see clouds that look like a piece of cotton. In your mind, you're thinking that this is the closest view to a heavenly place. What a beautiful sight that brings tranquility.

You are twenty minutes away from landing, and out of nowhere, turbulence comes. It's an automatic reaction for many to panic, but in your mind, you were just meditating on the plane because of your heavenly view. So, you have two options. You can join in with the panic of everyone else, or you can stay in that place of peace and assurance in your mind and spirit. You know that no matter what happens in your transition from one place to the next, you will make it through the rocky turbulence.

> *Those who entwine their hearts with Yahweh will experience divine strength. They will rise up on soaring wings and fly like eagles, run their race without*

growing weary, and walk through life without giving up.

— ISAIAH 40:31

My King, My Lord, create in me a clean heart and renew a right spirit within me. Let my heart and spirit become one with You, today. I come in agreement with heaven, and I receive Your divine strength. I shall not stagger on the promises of God or waver in my faith, for my trust is in You. It is through You that I ascend to the highest peaks of Your glory to stand in heavenly places— strong and secure in You (Psalm 18:33).

I am empowered, today, to walk in victory, as You have promised, for the battle has already been won. You have conquered the world (John 16:33), so I shall not fear the turbulence. As I soar above the rough stages of life, I know that I can find refuge under Your wings (Psalm 91:4). As You are seated on the throne, I am seated in heavenly places, in the glorious perfection and authority of the heavenly realm, being one with Christ (Ephesians 2:6). In Jesus' Name. Amen.

* * *

Take a moment to think, reflect, pray, and meditate. As you are praying, God will begin to highlight what to write regarding what's needed in your life to move forward according to His will.

Reflect/Journal

Day 10

RIDING THE WAVES

Imagine yourself at the beach. Can you smell the scent of the salt as you approach the shallow water on a hot, sunny day? Can you feel the water coming over you, pushed by every wave of the sea? When you look at God's creation, you may say to yourself that only a divine being could've done this. You may look out to see the vast sea that goes as far as your eyes can see, as if there is no end in sight. It may leave you in amazement, as you begin to walk out into the deeper water. The waves may start coming in stronger and higher. To those who aren't familiar with the power of a wave or what they wave are, waves are moved by wind, as well as the gravitational pull of the sun, moon, and earth. It is important to be watchful and notice when the waves form, and are coming your way. The waves in life aren't meant to overtake you. God intends to use them to show you your ability in Him. You will be able to see something that has the ability to stop you, but instead, elevates you. So, don't be consumed by the waves that you see, for we serve a God that the winds and waves obey. We won't be blindsided by anything that we face in life because we walk by faith and not by sight.

When you pass through the deep, stormy sea, you count on Me to be there with you. When you pass through the raging rivers, you will not drown.

— ISAIAH 43:2

. . .

My beloved Father, My Protector, I am grateful to serve You and know that You have my best interest at heart. Whatever comes my way, I know that it does not have the ability to overtake me, because You are with me. Everywhere I go, You're there. So, I shall not fear. Fear is not a part of my life. Your perfect love has destroyed its agenda.

Father, I pray that the wave of glory that You are sending my way today will drown out fear and doubt. I will not look at the obstacle, but instead, focus on You. I pray for stability, as the winds blow, and the sail of the boat catches the wind to keep going. I pray that the wind of God will give me consistent flow through the rain, hail, snow, turbulence, and anything sent to cause me to jump ship or abort my destiny.

I thank You, Father, for the boldness that is being developed during this time of igniting. I will no longer be the same, as a change is taking place. That change is marvelous in Your eyes. Today is a new day, and I open my heart for change. In Jesus' Name. Amen.

* * *

Take a moment to think, reflect, pray, and meditate. As you are praying, God will begin to highlight what to write regarding what's needed in your life to move forward according to His will.

REVIVE, REFRESH, RENEW

Reflect/Journal

Day 11
LOVE THE PAIN AWAY

What is the true definition of love? God is love. In 1 John 4:8, it says, "Anyone who does not love does not know God, because God is love."

> *Love is patient and kind. Love is not jealous or boastful or proud or rude. It does not demand its own way. It is not irritable, and it keeps no record of being wronged. It does not rejoice about injustice but rejoices whenever the truth wins out. Love never gives up, never loses faith, is always hopeful, and endures through every circumstance.*
>
> —1 CORINTHIANS 13:4–7

His character is who He is and what He does— in Word and deed. God is also the following:

- Omnipotent = All-Powerful
- Self-Existing = God has no beginning or end
- Self-Sufficient = God has life in Himself (John 5:26)
- Just = Brings moral equity to everyone

- Immutable = God never changes and is the same yesterday, today, and forever more
- Merciful = Actively compassionate to His people
- Eternal = God always has been, and will forever be, in eternity
- Omnipresent = Always present; He is everywhere

. . .

"Love covers a multitude of sins" (1 Pet. 4:8). True love is unconditional. Sometimes, when your heart is so full of pain, it's hard to receive it. Love is not forceful; it will wait until we are ready to receive it. The Giver of life, the One and True Almighty God, knows where to release and also how to break our walls down. Only God can change the heart of man.

In order for the pain to go away, you have to first acknowledge that you're in pain. It seems like this wouldn't be an issue because you want it to go away. But some believe it's easier not to deal with the sting of it and run, pretending that the pain isn't there. Love has the power to heal and help in your recovery from the painful wounds that you experience in your life. There is no traumatizing experience that will exceed God's ability to heal.

> *Father God, I pray that I experience more of Your love. Please help me to respond differently to the love that transcends far beyond what I can see or even understand. I ask You to erase that false perception that I have of love, so that I receive Your genuine love. I thank You for Your unconditional love that You have shown me throughout my life; Your love covers a multitude of all my sins. I don't ever have to be reminded of anything from my past because after I am forgiven, You remember it no more. I pray that every barrier that I have around the chambers of my heart be torn down, so that You can bring healing and restoration. I breathe in the breath of life, and I*

release every anxiety that would cause me to lack peace and fulfillment of Your love. In Jesus' Name. Amen.

* * *

Take a moment to think, reflect, pray, and meditate. As you are praying, God will begin to highlight what to write regarding what's needed in your life to move forward according to His will.

Reflect/Journal

Day 12
THE WALK ALONE

Being alone and being lonely are not the same. Sometimes, in life, we may feel alienated from others because we may feel like we don't fit in. What gives us the initial inclination that others don't accept who we are? Verbal messages and body language can be indicators. Our thoughts of insecurity can make us feel less confident around others who appear different, or those who may have more materialistically or intellectually. Even in these areas, it's all about perception. The way people act and react to life are often based on the foundation of who they are. You can put two people in a room from two different backgrounds to handle a certain scenario, and they both may see it and respond to it differently.

The lenses of our mind can make us feel that we are alone and not accepted. But could it be a preconceived notion? Other parties involved could possibly be thinking the same thing. All of these emotions can cause us to retreat, and oftentimes, it's for the wrong reasons: fear of hurt, fear of rejection, fear of abandonment, etc. Time by yourself doesn't have to be for these reasons. Time alone can simply be a time to refresh and reassess.

There were many times that Jesus went away to pray and recoup, but not because of fear. He needed to get away from the noise. From a humanistic view, life can sometimes appear to be a walk alone. However, we must remember that God our Father never leaves us.

CRYSTAL LOVE

. . .

*The Lord Himself goes before you and will be with you;
He will never leave you nor forsake you. Do not be
afraid; do not be discouraged.*

— DEUTERONOMY 31:8

Times When Jesus Was Alone

*Very early in the morning, while it was still dark, Jesus
got up, left the house and went off to a solitary place,
where He prayed.*

— MARK 1:35

* Everyone was looking for Jesus, but after His time in prayer, He told His disciples that it was time for them to move on to another village.

*[Despite Jesus's plea that His miracles be kept secret] the
news about him spread all the more, so that crowds of
people came to hear him and to be healed of their sicknesses. But Jesus often withdrew to lonely places and
prayed.*

— LUKE 5:15–16, SEE ALSO MARK 1:45

When Jesus heard [that John the Baptist had been

beheaded], he withdrew by boat privately to a solitary place.

— MATTHEW 14:13

Because so many people were coming and going that they did not even have a chance to eat, [Jesus] said to [his disciples], "Come with me by yourselves to a quiet place and get some rest." So they went away by themselves in a boat to a solitary place.

— MARK 6:31–32

After [Jesus] had dismissed [the crowds], he went up on a mountainside by himself to pray. When evening came, he was [still] there alone.

— MATTHEW 14:23, SEE ALSO MARK 6:46

Father, in the Name of Jesus, today I know that because You are with me, I am never alone. You promised in Your Word to never leave me, and I know that I am never alone. I ask that You help me. Even in those moments when I feel distant from You, You are always there. I pray that You fill the empty places with Your love, peace, joy, and contentment, so that no matter who leaves or stays, I don't react to life out of feelings of loneliness. Help me to understand that in some seasons in my life, I will not always have people around, and I can be confident in knowing that these times are necessary, so that I can draw closer to You. In Jesus' Name. Amen.

* * *

Take a moment to think, reflect, pray, and meditate. As you are praying, God will begin to highlight what to write regarding what's needed in your life to move forward according to His will.

REVIVE, REFRESH, RENEW

Reflect/Journal

Day 13
ENCOURAGE YOURSELF

Validation from others feels good at the moment, but you cannot depend on this for survival. You can't depend on the applause of anyone to make you feel positive about what God created you to be. What happens when the praise of people stop?

We have built up our expectation from others' opinions to form our character. This causes us to be in a place where we are afraid and maybe even reluctant to move forward in confidence. Do you stop because the applause stops? Do you stay motivated when no one is cheering you on, and telling you that you can make it?

Sometimes you will get criticized, and sometimes you will be spoken well of, but this cannot be the gauge from which you operate and live your life. In those times of despair (yes— they come), you may feel like asking, "What's the point? Why do I continue? Will change come?" Yes, indeed it will!

Speak life, even in those moments when things are intense and don't seem to be working in your favor. God is setting the stage for a great victory that you could not have anticipated. Lift up your head because the glory is here. God's presence is with you and will guide you into all truth.

David was greatly distressed because the men were talking of stoning him; each one was bitter in spirit because of

> *his sons and daughters. But David found strength in the LORD his God.*
>
> — 1 SAMUEL 30:6

> *Father God, in Jesus' Name, I thank You for the Holy Spirit that makes intercession for us. When we don't know what to pray, He takes over and speaks through us. I thank You, Father, that You are there all the time, even in times when I feel like I can't trace You. I pray that no matter what comes or goes, that I will add to my faith, the patience to wait until change comes. I know that Your timing is perfect, and though, in my eyes it may be delayed, I know that I'm right on Your divine schedule. I declare that I will walk in courage in the midst of adversity. I will embrace change when it is inevitable. I will speak life when everything may appear to be stagnant. The power of life and death are in the power of my own tongue. So, I take authority under the Blood of Jesus Christ that every promise shall manifest in my life. In Jesus' Name. Amen.*

> *Likewise, the Spirit helps in our weakness. For we do not know what to pray for as we ought, but the Spirit himself intercedes for us with groanings too deep for words.*
>
> — ROMANS 8:26

* * *

Take a moment to think, reflect, pray, and meditate. As you are praying, God will begin to highlight what to write regarding what's needed in your life to move forward according to His will.

REVIVE, REFRESH, RENEW

Reflect/Journal

Day 14
NAIL THE TARGET

What are nails used for? They are small metal spikes with a broadened flat head, driven typically into wood with a hammer to join things together or to serve as a peg or hook.

Many of us are typically trying to get from point A to point B in life. This is the point where both ends meet. But how they meet is based upon you bringing those two ends together. The earth would just be an empty space if we weren't here to fill it and bring things together.

In the construction of a building, nails are used to hold pieces of wood together to establish a frame for the building. Nothing else can be done until the foundation and the frame are finished. We now have something to build upon. Nails are nothing unless you have something strong and firm to nail them to. Some surfaces cannot handle the hammering of a nail, let alone the nail itself, so more sensitive adhesive has to be applied to piece those two ends together.

We don't know what will happen from one destination to the next, but our focus at that moment is to get there— efficiently! None of us would volunteer for a slow ride if we are in a hurry. How can we gauge our pace? Our pace can be affected by the company we keep, what we watch, or who we pay attention to. To make sense of all this, allow me to drive this point home.

It's finally the time to finalize some things that have been floating in the air. It's time to seal the deal on some ideas, dreams, and goals that have just been a thought and never put into action. You must pray, plan, and execute. Name one target that you would like to focus on in the next coming weeks and mark today as the day to start. Write out your plan and pray for strategy regarding how to *nail the target*. In order to hit the target, you have to properly focus and aim. It will take much practice and sometimes some errors, but always try.

> *Thus, all the work of Solomon was carried out from the day of the foundation of the house of the LORD, and until it was finished. So the house of the LORD was completed.*
>
> — 2 CHRONICLES 8:16

> *So he built the house and finished it; and he covered the house with beams and planks of cedar.*
>
> — 1 KINGS 6:9

> *Father God, I know that in times past, I have missed many targets and have not been able to hone in on what mattered the most. But today, I ask You to forgive me for living with the guilt, shame, and regrets from the past. I know that according to Your Word that all things work together for the good of those who love the Lord and are called according to His purpose. So, today, I choose to walk in my divine purpose that You have mapped out for me. I thank You, Lord, for Your direction and guidance along the way. I seek Your wisdom, today. I thank You Lord, for You are the Living Word. My prayer is to grow closer to You and be even more attentive to Your voice. You said in Your Word that Your sheep hear Your voice, and that a stranger they will not follow. So Lord,*

today, I choose to sit quietly to hear You clearly, follow your instructions, and obtain the victory in every area of my life that you promised was already mine. In Jesus' Name. Amen.

* * *

Take a moment to think, reflect, pray, and meditate. As you are praying, God will begin to highlight what to write regarding what's needed in your life to move forward according to His will.

Reflect/Journal

Day 15
FIGHT OPPOSITION

Opposition comes when there is something of great value on the horizon. Look at the story of Nehemiah, and how he had such a great burden to help the Israelites rebuild the walls of Jerusalem. Jerusalem was once a defensed city. In Old Testament times, the city walls represented not only the strength of the people within that city, but also the strength of the God they served. The people were weary, distracted, and took their focus off God. Nehemiah led the initiative to rebuild the Walls of Jerusalem.

The Wall of Answered Prayer represents the strength of God. Jerusalem is a symbol of the City of God, God's dwelling place, and the center of life for the world. The strength of God and the people are represented by the walls. He promptly made his famous night journey around the city, surveying the dilapidated city wall (Nehemiah 2:11–15). He gathered all the men of Israel to rebuild the walls, and though Nehemiah and his team faced significant opposition, they were able to rebuild the city walls in just fifty-two days. This was a miraculous accomplishment that was a monument to God's glory and faithfulness, as depicted in Nehemiah 6:15–16. The people of Jerusalem were deeply inspired by him.

We have confidence in knowing that God has already obtained the victory for us. He is the victory. So, today, make the choice to let Him be your perfect Defender. He wants you to focus on His divine plan for your life, submit yourself to Him, and resist the devil so that the enemy will leave. Whenever faced with opposition, just remember to pick up your weapon— the Sword of the Spirit and the Word of God will do the work (Ephesians 6:17).

When Jesus was tempted in the wilderness by Satan, He used the Word of God and declared, "It is written." And if God wrote it and said it, then it's already done and settled. All you have to do is believe and receive by faith. Remember, faith comes by hearing the Word of God (Romans 10:17). We must cast down, destroy, and dismiss every thought that exalts itself against the knowledge of God (2 Corinthians 10:5). Now, this lets us know that we have to know and study the Bible in order to use it in our spiritual battle.

> *And they said, Let us rise up and build.*
>
> — NEHEMIAH 2:18

> *"Now behold, I have made you today as a fortified city and as a pillar of iron and as walls of bronze against the whole land, to the kings of Judah, to its princes, to its priests and to the people of the land. They will fight against you, But they shall not prevail against you. For I am with you," says the Lord, "to deliver you."*
>
> — JEREMIAH 1:18–19

When we build the people, we build the walls and fortify the city. In Ephesians 2:17–22, the body of Christ is described like the walls of a temple "built on the foundation of the apostles and prophets, with Christ Jesus Himself as the cornerstone" (verse 20). We are all part of the wall that "grows into a holy sanctuary in the Lord" (verse 21). In an individual's life, then, the rebuilding of the walls would be a picture of reestablishing the strength of your life.

> *My Father, You're the Creator of all things. I know that You have already won every battle that I face in my*

life. I know that the battle is not mine; it is Yours. I have faith in knowing that You have already overcome the world, so I can receive the peace of God. Your peace will release me from every anxiety that will try to infiltrate my mind. So today, I receive Your strength to continue every task that is set before me. And I will use the Sword of the Spirit, which is the Word of God, for any temptation that may come my way to take my focus off of You. In Jesus' Name, I pray. Amen.

* * *

Take a moment to think, reflect, pray, and meditate. As you are praying, God will begin to highlight what to write regarding what's needed in your life to move forward according to His will.

Reflect/Journal

Day 16

NO LONGER HIDDEN

I have boxes stacked up in my basement. They are packed full of various items. I have them labeled so that I know where to find what I want to retrieve, when needed. Unfortunately, several boxes fell over one day, and all of what was in one box began to come out. This box was worn out from every day wear and tear— from being moved from place to place. As a result, I had to take the things out and place them somewhere else, because the box could no longer contain what was in it. The contents in the box was also packaged in plastic wrap.

Whatever we have been carrying from season to season or place to place, without using it, is now ready to be used. Now is the time to get it out and use what has been stored away.

God wants to remind us of what we have stored away and have forgotten about. It is time to use it now. It was bought with a price. It's costly and can't go to waste. Instead of using what is new for a new season, we have been taking things that are old and adding a little bit of the new. Just like a refurbished phone, we tried to fix it and package it into a new package. When in fact, it's faulty and is not able to deliver to its fullest capacity.

God is currently stirring up people who will receive information from Him and use it. It's 'due' season, and it's 'now' time. We need fresh manna from heaven, fresh off the press. The Gospel of Jesus Christ is good news, not old news packaged differently. Let's practice a life of obedience to what He has released to us. Some things must happen in their proper time; everything that God gives us now may not be for now. He will, first, test and prepare you before you can release what He has given you.

Jesus came to earth both divine and human, to show us the process of life and how we are to carry out our God-given purpose on earth. He came through a supernatural conception, as Mary went through the process of a natural birth. Her baby had to mature, learn, and grow.

Life is an adventurous journey to walk out through faith with God. Take advantage of every opportunity to learn of God and allow Him to transform you. Share your testimony with others so that they can experience the freedom from bondage to sin, and the liberty of living a life fashioned for them, in truth.

THE LIFE OF JESUS

- **Birth** (Matthew 1-2; Luke 2)
- **Baptism** (Matthew 3:13-17; Mark 1:9-11; Luke 3:21-23)
- **First Miracle** (John 2:1-11)
- **Sermon on the Mount** (Matthew 5:1-7:29)
- **Feeding of the 5,000** (Matthew 14:15-21; Mark 6:34-44; Luke 9:12-17; John 6:5-13)
- **Transfiguration** (Matthew 17:1-8; Mark 9:2-18; Luke 9:26-36)
- **Raising of Lazarus** (John 11:1-44)
- **Triumphal Entry** (Matthew 21:1-11, 14-17; Mark 11:1-11; Luke 19:29-44; John 12:12-19)
- **Last Supper** (Matthew 26:1-30; Mark 14:12-26; Luke 22:7-38; John 13:1-38)
- **Arrest at Gethsemane** (Matthew 26:36-56; Mark 14:32-50; Luke 22:39-54; John 18:1-12)
- **Crucifixion and Burial** (Matthew 27:27-66; Mark 15:16-47; Luke 23:26-56; John 19:17-42)
- **Resurrection** (Matthew 28:1-10; Mark 16:1-11; Luke 24:1-12; John 20:1-10)

- **Post-Resurrection Appearances** (Matthew 28:1-20; Mark 16:1-20; Luke 24:1-53; John 20:1-21-25; Acts 1:3; 1 Corinthians 15:6)
- **Ascension** (Mark 16:19-20; Luke 24:50-53; Acts 1:9-12)

But we have this treasure in earthen vessels, that the excellency of the power may be of God, and not of us.

— 2 CORINTHIANS 4:7–10

Father God, I thank You for every treasure that You have imparted to me from the foundation of the world. I acknowledge that I may not know what You have called me to be in everything. But today, I make a declaration that I will submit my will to You, that Your will may be done in Jesus' Name. I draw nigh to You, and I pray for a deeper level of intimacy to be developed, as our relationship grows. For this treasure is not just for me, but it is for the glory of God to be revealed in the earth. My prayer is that others may see and feel Your love through my surrendered life. My prayer is that the exercising of my gifts will equip, bring knowledge, growth, and edification to the Body of Christ. For it is my responsibility to make sure that I do my part in the forward progression of the Body of Christ. In Jesus' Name I pray. Amen.

* * *

Take a moment to think, reflect, pray, and meditate. As you are praying, God will begin to highlight what to write regarding what's needed in your life to move forward according to His will.

Reflect/Journal

Day 17
A NEW DAY IS DAWNING

Separation means to keep apart, or to set aside for a special purpose. This can be temporary or permanent. In order to separate, this means that there was first a joining together— unity. Unity refers to something joined, whether it was intentional or not. It's an important topic that needs to be addressed. When you are in a relationship with someone, or in a marriage, you both had something in common that helped you get to this place. There was something that sparked the interest.

In order to walk in the now, we have let go of what has happened in the past. Take a moment and think about what you have been through and say to yourself that it's definitely time for something different.

I often think about the first time that I traveled out of the country on a cruise. I was so accustomed to seeing water filled with debris that when I saw the water in the middle of the ocean, it was so clear and blue that I thought to myself, "This can't be real!" I felt like I had been deprived from seeing God's creations. So, after that day, I was determined to travel the world.

One of the ways for your mindset to shift to something new is to be exposed to something new. We, sometimes, get so accustomed to the normal routine. For example, we may cross the same stoplights every day or drive around the same neighborhoods, and never get exposed to a new way of living. We don't know that there's more to life because we haven't always had options.

You have options; there is more! Do you want more? More is available for you!

> *See, I am doing a new thing! Now it springs up; do you not perceive it? I am making a way in the wilderness and streams in the wasteland.*
>
> — ISAIAH 43:19

Father, in the Name of Jesus, I declare that today is a new day! I will no longer think the same. I will be transformed by the renewing of my mind, washing daily in the Word. Everything about my future is new, refreshing, promising, and will be impactful to whoever's life I come in contact with. My purpose is greater than me. Greater is He that is in me than he that is in the world. I shall not be ashamed to show the love of God to a dying world. My new life and new beginning will cause others to dream again. Lord, let my heart's desire line up with Your will for my life in Jesus' Name. Amen.

✳ ✳ ✳

Take a moment to think, reflect, pray, and meditate. As you are praying, God will begin to highlight what to write regarding what's needed in your life to move forward according to His will.

Reflect/Journal

Day 18

DON'T MISS THE MOMENT

We have to stay alert and focused. Don't miss this moment—the moment to build your life, develop structure, and gain momentum. Let your plan for your life be at the forefront of your mind, daily. Daily, seek God first, and remain open to visions, as He always reveals truth. He has informed us by saying, "I want my people to flourish, but they have to walk in the spirit and obey my command."

Obedience leads to favor, prosperity, health, family, ministry, and business. Our relationships with God are based on instructions. We receive instructions in order to have structure. God organizes our lives so that we can have structure in the midst of chaos. This is what God did in seven days; He spoke things into existence, and inside everything spoken were instructions, tasks, and purpose. A product without instructions will be used improperly and will be wasted. We can't just know our purpose; we have to know how God wants us to walk out our purpose.

We must have daily communion and receive the Word of God as our daily bread. Fresh manna is what God sent the Israelites in the wilderness, as they were headed toward the Promised Land. We can't use yesterday's instructions for today's assignment. Every day serves a purpose. He told the Israelites to eat what was assigned to them for that day, and throw the rest away. God always gives us more than enough. In other words, we can't live in our past and continue to plan for the future. Tomorrow will take care of itself. Yield every day its fruit.

Every day, we are being washed in the Word of God with clean hands. Drown out negative thoughts, suffocate fears, remove the pain of yesterday, and walk in the healing of today. Imagine yourself going to the basement, getting something that you weren't looking for that you forgot was there, while searching for something else. God will reveal more to you when you're consistently seeking Him. Your life will make sense. The more you learn of Him, the more He shows you yourself, because you are His reflection in the earth.

Like Jesus said, "I do the works of My Father who sent me. When you see Me, you see My Father." This is how children should follow Jesus. Our foundation should be based on our fellowship with God, prayer, the Word of God, and communion with Him.

- Identity Discovered
- Purpose Revealed
- Instructions Needed
- Work Applied
- Results Yielded
- Reproduce and Multiply

> *Father God, I am approaching You like the children of Israel that were released from the bondage of Egypt. Sometimes, my thoughts try to keep me in a place of delay and captivity. However, I am determined to enter into all of what You have promised me. Just as Moses prepared the people to enter and Joshua led them, so shall the Holy Spirit lead and guide me into all truth. I shall live to see the glory of God revealed in my life. I pray, also, for others who may be struggling today, because their present situations may not always demonstrate what You said. But we know that it's*

coming! It may not come as we expect, but we know it's on the way.

Father God, You are not a man that You should lie, so I trust every truth that You have spoken over me, and I declare that it shall come to pass. In Jesus' Name, I pray. Amen.

* * *

Take a moment to think, reflect, pray, and meditate. As you are praying, God will begin to highlight what to write regarding what's needed in your life to move forward according to His will.

Reflect/Journal

Day 19
LET GO... LET FLOW

Holding on to something for so long out of fear, and not releasing it to allow it to flow, can hold you back. There should not always be a negative approach to this. This can be an idea, invention, ministry, or project of any sort. First, it may come to you as a thought in your mind. Then, you may begin to analyze and wonder how you can get it done. Let go of insecurities. When we feel like we are incapable of doing something, God our Creator is able to do the rest. If we present ourselves (including our gifts) to Him and consult Him for the next instructions, our limited mindset will be a distant memory.

We don't have to depend on our known abilities when there is more to us than what we see or perceive. Write down the first thing that comes to mind that is stopping your flow of life. What have you done to stop the flow? What can you do more or less of for the flow to continue, be stronger, and effective?

> Father, I pray today that everything that has stopped me from moving forward with visions and ideas will no longer be a hindrance. I will not be blinded by my inadequacies. I choose to let the past, my thoughts, and insecurities go! I choose to take my own brakes and

> *limits off, so that You can flow freely through me with Your love, power, strength, and abilities. For I am Your child, made in the likeness of Your image. I resemble You because You are my Father. I receive the rights that I have to receive in the family of God. I thank God for my natural parents that you chose to give birth to me naturally, but now I have been born again. I am born with new life, free from sin and death. And now I can live in eternal life with Your eternal promises, while living an abundant life. In Jesus' Name. Amen.*

> *Now there was a man of the Pharisees named Nicodemus, a ruler of the Jews. This man came to Jesus by night and said to Him, "Rabbi, we know that you are a teacher come from God, for no one can do these signs that you do unless God is with him."*
> *Jesus answered him, "Truly, truly, I say to you, unless one is born again he cannot see the kingdom of God."*
> *Nicodemus said to Him, "How can a man be born when he is old? Can he enter a second time into his mother's womb and be born?"*
> *Jesus answered, "Truly, truly, I say to you, unless one is born of water and the Spirit, he cannot enter the kingdom of God."*
>
> — JOHN 3:1–5

Nicodemus' encounter with Jesus changed his life, forever. Though there may have seemed to be some resistance, Jesus gave Him understanding of what he was about to walk into. He just needed to know that being born again was possible, or even necessary.

Being "born of water," to be baptized in water, being "born again of the Spirit." Water baptism is a part of the born-again experience, but it alone cannot wash away our sins. However, this can be made possible through the Blood of Jesus and what He did on the Cross.

Salvation in the Spirit

To be born again of the Spirit is to invite Jesus into one's being, verbally. The Holy Spirit of God then enters and abides within the Believer.

Water Baptism

To confirm and signify that rebirth, the new Believer is baptized in water in the Name of the Holy Spirit. This baptism is known as the Christian baptism.

That which is born of the flesh is flesh, and that which is born of the Spirit is spirit.

— JOHN 3:16

God is three persons in One: God the Father, God the Son, and God the Holy Spirit.

And he said unto me, My grace is sufficient for thee: for my strength is made perfect in weakness.

— 2 CORINTHIANS 12:9

Father God, You have the grace to do what I don't have the ability to do in my natural strength. Today will be the start of renewed thinking, renewed strength, and the acceptance that You will complete the given tasks in my life.

. . .

> *Being confident of this very thing, that he which hath begun a good work in you will perform it until the day of Jesus Christ.*
>
> — PHILIPPIANS 1:6

* * *

Take a moment to think, reflect, pray, and meditate. As you are praying, God will begin to highlight what to write regarding what's needed in your life to move forward according to His will.

REVIVE, REFRESH, RENEW

Reflect/Journal

Day 20
PROMISED POTENTIAL

Do you realize that you have great potential to accomplish everything that God has created you to do? All of us have the potential to produce and reproduce. Potential generally refers to a currently unrealized ability. You have many seeds, but are they being watered and nurtured? This has been promised to us; therefore, it will be produced.

Examine the relationships that you're in now. Will they help you move forward in the next phase of your life? There are specific details about each of us that can indicate our potential. Some may have the ability to take a machine, examine every detail of it, and know how to fix it when there is a problem without going to school to learn about it. This is an ability that you have that you were born with; you just sometimes don't know it's there. It is important to continue to go back to our source. As a matter of fact, stay connected always to the source of our life and everything that it pertains to. Our Father in heaven is our source. We thank Him for allowing His Spirit— Himself in the person of the Holy Spirit— to live on the inside of us.

We realize that everything cannot be given at one time because it cannot be processed or digested all in one time period. We have to receive it, process it, and then apply it for a particular season. Then, we can move on to the next phase. Sometimes, we may get stuck at the receiving part; we may not be able to receive because we don't believe. If you don't believe in the information, then it won't be received, and this is because sometimes we lack trust in our divine source. When you believe in the source, you will be unstoppable. Everything that the source releases will be received and applied. We have to commit to the process.

Just imagine God having a packet on the table, and He said, "In this packet is the blueprint of your life, but you have to commit, be devoted, and dedicated to daily training in order for the plan to work." In response, you may say to yourself, "How am I supposed to manage the rest of my life?" This packet will help you manage your entire life. There is no life outside of God's plan that will prosper. The only thing outside of God's plan is our plan, and that has to be dismissed.

> *"For I know the plans I have for you," declares the LORD, "plans to prosper you and not to harm you, plans to give you hope and a future."*
>
> *— JEREMIAH 29:11*

> *Father God, I pray today that every plan that You have for my life will be revealed to me. I pray that in the days, weeks, and months to come, I will be more drawn to You in my prayers and devotion to my purpose. I submit totally to Your will for my life, and, Lord, forgive me for not totally believing my ability to produce what You have placed in me.*
>
> *Father, help my unbelief. I know that the plans that You have for me are plans to prosper me and not to harm me— plans to give me hope and a future. Today, I embrace my hope, and pray that it be restored. I pray that my future shall prosper according to the will of the Lord for my life. I will*

not give up, as the giver of life is flows through me. And even in my weakness, Your strength is made perfect. Your grace is sufficient for me, and I will trust in You wholly.

. . .

I believe; help my unbelief!

— MARK 9:24

He replied, "If you have faith as small as a mustard seed, you can say to this mulberry tree, 'Be uprooted and planted in the sea,' and it will obey you."

— LUKE 17:6

He replied, "Because you have so little faith. Truly I tell you, if you have faith as small as a mustard seed, you can say to this mountain, 'Move from here to there,' and it will move. Nothing will be impossible for you."

— MATTHEW 17:20

Even in those times of unbelief, help me to stand on the promises written in the Word of God to increase my faith.

So then faith cometh by hearing, and hearing by the Word of God.

— ROMANS 10:17

But he said to me, "My grace is sufficient for you, for my power is made perfect in weakness." Therefore I will

> *boast all the more gladly about my weaknesses, so that Christ's power may rest on me.*
>
> — 2 CORINTHIANS 12:9

* * *

Take a moment to think, reflect, pray, and meditate. As you are praying, God will begin to highlight what to write regarding what's needed in your life to move forward according to His will.

Reflect/Journal

Day 21
FAITHFUL PROOF

Some people need proof— proof for everything. Some desire proof in order to believe. If you are pursuing a business, it's okay to have proof. God doesn't mind proving Himself. There are some things that will be done, and we will know that He is God.

Let's discuss the Samaritan woman at the well. Jesus had a divine appointment with this lady that changed the course of her life and the lives of those in her culture. There was a clash with the Jews and the Samaritans. The Samaritans in the Bible would mix what they wanted as it pertains to their own cultural beliefs and personal opinions along with the law of God as it pertains to what God released to Moses. This was a problem with the Jews because while they served the Lord and totally depended on the foundation of truth, they were offended and did defend the Gospel. On one occasion, they burned down the temple that the Samaritans had erected to worship.

Jesus wanted to bridge the gap between the Jews and the Samaritans. Among the Samaritans, there were some who still needed to hear the Gospel of Jesus Christ, and God was going to use the Samaritan woman to bridge that gap.

We will find in life that with unity, we can get more accomplished and be effective and efficient in ways that we can never imagine. Jesus spoke to her past, present, and future— bringing healing and restoration in her life.

Have you ever had an encounter with God that was pivotal and changed your life?

> *My loving Father, I thank You for today and the memories that I have of the past times where I felt like I needed proof. While my faith may have not been in operation, in spite of doubt, You still made me aware that You heard the cries of my heart. And in response, this ignited another level of faith and trust in You. My prayer today is that by hearing the spoken Word and reading the written Word, that I will believe You for any present situations I am facing, and trust that anything You have spoken is and shall be, whether I see a sign or not.*
>
> *I know that You will continue to show that You are God in the earth and in the lives of others, but this will not be the basis from which I believe in You. I pray that as I continue to commune with You, my faith will increase (2 Peter 1:4–10). For You have given me very great and precious promises, so that through them, I may participate in the divine nature, having escaped the corruption in the world caused by evil desires.*
>
> *So Father, by Your grace, I will make every effort to add to my faith goodness; and to goodness, knowledge; and to knowledge, self-control; and to self-control, perseverance; and to perseverance, godliness; and to godliness, mutual affection; and to mutual affection, love. For if I possess these qualities in increasing measure, they will keep me from being ineffective and unproductive in my knowledge of You, Lord. Amen.*

* * *

Take a moment to think, reflect, pray, and meditate. As you are praying, God will begin to highlight what to write regarding what's needed in your life to move forward according to His will.

Reflect/Journal

Day 22
IDENTITY CRISIS

The world calls it branding. The world is having an identity crisis. We are all searching to figure out where we sit. We fashion ourselves according to watching others, because that's how we learn how to do most of what we do. As a baby, we emulate others and seek their guidance until we get mature enough to know right from wrong. Then, we can make our own decisions based upon who we are as a person, and not based on how others think we should be.

Well, it is different with God. He is our Father. He made us in His image. All of us are His children. Though we all look different in appearance and character, we all have a common denominator, and that is to spread the Good News amid the evil all around. We must be the light of God in darkness. People are walking around blindfolded in life, searching for answers and clarity. They hear and see something in the midst of this. It's shining brighter than any form of light that they have seen, and it's speaking louder than any voice that they have heard.

When I was led to go to strangers and minister to them, most of the time it was not foreign to them. It was confirmation of what they were sensing and needed to hear. The harvest is ripe, ready for us to go out and get it. If you put all of what you are in a package— a package of what you want the world to see— you are Jesus branded.

To know who we are, we must know our Creator as the only true and living God. Father, help us start on that journey. Father God, show me myself. Illuminate my eyes to see the wonderful things on the path to the promises of God. Everything that You have planned for my life, I will walk in it with confidence and readiness. No weapon formed against me shall prosper for the promises are God and are yes and amen. If it is written and spoken, it shall manifest. I shall see the salvation of the Lord in the land of the living. Nothing shall separate me from the love of God. I shall stand my ground and walk in the authority of God. I shall not live beneath what my Father has purposed for me. I am a Child of God, and I receive my divine inheritance. I am accepted into the family of God, and I have the spiritual backing and support. I am not an orphan, but I am a child of the King, the King of kings, the Lord of lords. In Jesus' Name, I pray. Amen.

"No weapon forged against you will prevail, and you will refute every tongue that accuses you. This is the heritage of the servants of the LORD, and this is their vindication from me," declares the LORD.

— ISAIAH 54:17

God decided in advance to adopt us into his own family by bringing us to himself through Jesus Christ. God made a choice to take us in, granting us a new start in the wonderful family of God. The Lord took on the responsibilities of a parent—protecting us, providing for us, nurturing us and guiding us.

— EPHESIANS 1:5

* * *

Take a moment to think, reflect, pray, and meditate. As you are praying, God will begin to highlight what to write regarding what's needed in your life to move forward according to His will.

Reflect/Journal

Day 23

UNDERSTANDING THE SEASON

What are you loyal, dedicated, and faithful to? What has your undivided attention on a daily basis? What is the first thing that is on your mind when you wake up? And what is the last thing on your mind when you go to sleep?

When you are devoted to something, nothing can get in the way. This particular person or thing will always have your undivided attention. Circumstances may come to try to sway your mind and attention away from your devotion. Nothing, by any means, can stop you from making this devotion your priority. Maybe it's something that you want to be more devoted to you, and you just don't know how to handle that situation. On the other hand, God may know that you need to be more devoted to a specific situation, person, or thing, but everything else has your attention.

Well, today is the day that we pray, and we make a commitment to devote ourselves to this particular thing a person. It's just a matter of making a decision. One factor you have to keep in mind is that you cannot devote yourself to the wrong thing. So, you have to question the thing that you want to devote and give more time to. Will this thing or person have a good or bad effect on every other area of your life?

You can create a list of pros and cons regarding the areas that have your devotion. Make one column for devotions, one column for benefits, one column for negative possibilities, and one column for positive or negative effects.

Things You're Devoted To	Benefits	Negative Possibilities	Positive/Negative Effects

Father, in the name of Jesus, You are in control of the times and seasons. I pray that today I open my mind, body, and spirit to Your timing. Though there are many things that You have revealed to me, I need to know what You would like me to produce in this season for the steps of a righteous man are ordered by You.

I thank You, Father, that I have been justified and declared righteous by the Blood of Jesus. And I shall not be double-minded, but be stable in every way, according to the power of the Holy Spirit that works through me. May Your will for my life, ministry, and family be accomplished in this season, so that I may be in full alignment with the Word of God that has been spoken and written. My ways are not Your ways, and my thoughts are not Yours. So, today I choose to come into divine covenant with You, Father, for Your will for my life to be accomplished in Jesus' Name, I pray. Amen.

. . .

The steps of a good man are ordered by the LORD: and he delighteth in his way.

— PSALM 37:23

A double minded man is unstable in all his ways.

— JAMES 1:8

That being justified by his grace, we should be made heirs according to the hope of eternal life.

— TITUS 3:7

Therefore being justified by faith, we have peace with God through our Lord Jesus Christ.

— ROMANS 5:1

* * *

Take a moment to think, reflect, pray, and meditate. As you are praying, God will begin to highlight what to write regarding what's needed in your life to move forward according to His will.

Reflect/Journal

Day 24
TIMING IS PERFECT

Use your time wisely. Time is priceless. Time costs, although you don't physically pay for it. However, if you are providing a service to someone, you can be paid for the time spent for the service rendered. But what about those who give their time to people and things, and never get payment for it? This question is in reference to wasted time. It's okay to spend time doing something that later in life will bring you a return. If you invest your time and write a stage play, you can set up different stage plays all across the country and sell tickets and get a profit off it. This is time well spent.

If you spend time in prayer and communion with God, there are many priceless benefits from this. Not only will you develop a closer relationship with God, but you will also receive instruction regarding how to move forward in your life. Now, this is the number one most valuable way to spend your time. Spending time in the presence of the Lord will help you manage the rest of your time and all of the other areas. Managing time takes discipline and focus. Today, let's focus on better time management.

Father God, I know that You work in time, and that Your timing is perfect. I pray that during this time, I use the time that You have given me in the earth wisely. For according to Ecclesiastes, there is a time for everything.

To every thing there is a season, and a time to every purpose under the heaven: A time to be born, and a time to die; a time to plant, and a time to pluck up that which is planted; A time to kill, and a time to heal; a time to break down, and a time to build up; A time to weep, and a time to laugh; a time to mourn, and a time to dance; A time to cast away stones, and a time to gather stones together; a time to embrace, and a time to refrain from embracing; A time to get, and a time to lose; a time to keep, and a time to cast away; A time to rend, and a time to sew; a time to keep silence, and a time to speak; A time to love, and a time to hate; a time of war, and a time of peace.

— ECCLESIASTES 3:1–8

My prayer today is that I flow in Your time. What purpose does today serve? How much time would You like for me to spend with You? How much time should I spend with my family, etc.?

Lord, I pray for balance in every area. I pray for the divine assistance of my Father. I need You for time management so that I can arrive at every destination on time, prepared, and ready to complete every task. You are in control. I come into agreement with Your plan, in Jesus' Name. Amen.

* * *

Take a moment to think, reflect, pray, and meditate. As you are praying, God will begin to highlight what to write regarding what's needed in your life to move forward according to His will.

Reflect/Journal

Day 25
TAKE THE TIME TO HEAL

Relating to one another means having a common ground. It's so difficult and causes more hurt when you start something new when you're still attached to something old, even when you're unaware that the old thing is still there. You can go through life not even knowing that you are damaged— or causing yourself even more damage — by going in and out of relationships without healing. Time doesn't heal, but God's love can heal in time. *What does God's Word say about healing?*

> *Come to me, all you who are weary and burdened, and I will give you rest.*
>
> — MATTHEW 11:28

> *Lord my God, I called to you for help, and you healed me.*
>
> — PSALM 30:2

> *Surely he took up our pain and bore our suffering, yet we considered him punished by God, stricken by Him, and afflicted. But he was pierced for our transgres-*

> *sions, he was crushed for our iniquities; the punishment that brought us peace was on him, and by his wounds we are healed.*
>
> — ISAIAH 53:4–5

When there is a wound, it means something has been torn, and therefore, it allows other things to get in it. Before a Band-Aid is put on it, it has to be treated. We may try to convince ourselves after a breakup and say, "Oh well, I'll move on to the next." But that's not wise to do; the wound has to be treated first.

Feelings of abandonment, betrayal, hurt, disappointment, hope for a future, the fear of never finding love again, and fear of being alone can send us into a place of desperation. You want someone to feed that place. That place may be empty and starving to be filled again. You may take anything to fill this place. Your vision may not be clear because you still feel the pain. And sometimes when you feel pain, you are unable to make clear decisions.

> *Father God, I thank You for Your Word, as it brings us life. I pray that every truth come alive, be revealed, and yield its fruit. Let it produce freedom. May we put to death every lie for it is time to live. I declare that I will dwell and walk in Your truth. As the author and the finisher of our faith, You have orchestrated my life. You have written the book of my life. My book is already finished. For it is written that I am healed by your stripes. So, I declare today that I shall live and not die. I know that You had a plan for every experience in my life, even the ones that I didn't understand that caused me pain. You have worked it out for my good. I lay every wound of my heart at your feet, and today it's time for me to let go. I trade in my pain for Your joy for You are the lifter of my head. I will look unto the hills from whence comes my*

help; my help comes from You! And therefore, I will trust You. In Jesus' Name. Amen.

* * *

Take a moment to think, reflect, pray, and meditate. As you are praying, God will begin to highlight what to write regarding what's needed in your life to move forward according to His will.

Reflect/Journal

Day 26

DON'T SECOND-GUESS YOURSELF — DOUBT HAS TO GO

Do you second guess yourself? Do you struggle with trusting yourself? Is it hard for you to accept how God has created you?

> *But we have this treasure in earthen vessels, that the excellency of the power may be of God, and not of us*
>
> — 2 CORINTHIANS 4:7

> *Trust in the LORD with all your heart And do not lean on your own understanding.*
>
> — PROVERBS 3:5

I started off with these two Scriptures because we have to know that God has invested something very valuable inside of us, and we cannot second-guess it. We must trust in Him with all our heart. For us to do this, we have to believe in and yield to Him. Trust in His investment and allow His will to work through you. It will yield its fruit. We must water the garden of God with the Word of God so that we will continue to grow and be nurtured. There should be no trace of doubt when you are trusting God for anything. Pray in faith according to God's will, knowing that it will come to pass.

In order to trust with all your heart, it has to be yielded to the Lord. The question is: *How is this done? How do we allow God, through the person of the Holy Spirit, to be a part of every aspect of our lives?*

Our heart is the seat of our emotions, so this is where we hold everything we feel about all that we have experienced in life. Acknowledge your pain. This is not glorifying it. Rather, you are casting your cares on Him so that healing can take place. The Holy Spirit will reveal what needs to be addressed and healed in this season.

> *Without faith it is impossible to please God.*
>
> — HEBREWS 11:6

Father God, we thank You that today, I do not put my trust in man, and neither will I put my trust in myself. I put my trust in You, Lord. You are the author and the finisher of our faith. John 14:26 says, "But the Helper, the Holy Spirit, whom the Father will send in My Name, He will teach you all things and bring to your remembrance all that I have said to you." I will learn to trust Your voice. And as Your voice is getting clearer, the voices of fear and doubt will grow fainter the closer I get to You.

Lord, drown out every feeling of uncertainty and replace them with love, as it cancels out all fear. By Your stripes I am healed, and nothing from my past will delay anything in my future. I declare that every promise of God written in the Word of God will manifest in my life, and I will see the goodness of the Lord in the land of the living. In Jesus' Name. Amen.

There is no fear in love. But perfect love drives out fear, because fear has to do with punishment. The one who fears is not made perfect in love.

— JOHN 4:18

It is better to trust in the LORD than to put confidence in man.

— PSALM 118:8

For whoever wants to save their life will lose it, but whoever loses their life for me will find it. What good will it be for someone to gain the whole world, yet forfeit their soul? Or what can anyone give in exchange for their soul?

— MATTHEW 16:25–26

* * *

Take a moment to think, reflect, pray, and meditate. As you are praying, God will begin to highlight what to write regarding what's needed in your life to move forward according to His will.

Reflect/Journal

Day 27

I'M WINNING

We will never know the value of winning until we've lost. If you played any type of game in your life, it is so gratifying when you win. In that moment, you're not really concerned about the person who lost or even how they feel because your goal was to win. Who plays a game with the intention of losing? *No one!* Who runs a race saying to themselves, "I'm running this race to lose!" *No one!* You play to win, and you compete to win.

So, in this Christian race, the rewarding part about it is that the race is already won—the battle is already won. We just have to walk down the right path. It doesn't matter how fast you get there; just keep a steady pace in life, tracking your time, making progress, and learning along the way. So, no matter how you are feeling in a certain situation in your life, just know that you're winning regardless. We have victory in Jesus.

> *Father, in the Name of Jesus, we thank You for all the victories that we have seen in our lives and all the ones that we have yet to see (2 Chronicles 20:15). We know that the battle is not ours, it is Yours. You have already overcome the world, so we do not fear. You have not given us a spirit of fear, but of power, love, and of a sound mind. And because of that, we can*

rejoice (Romans 5:3). Also, we can glorify in tribulations, knowing that "tribulation worketh patience" (1 John 4:4). You, dear children, are from God and have overcome them because the One who is in you is greater than the one who is in the world (1 Corinthians 15:57). Thanks be to God! He gives us the victory through our Lord Jesus Christ. Amen.

* * *

Take a moment to think, reflect, pray, and meditate. As you are praying, God will begin to highlight what to write regarding what's needed in your life to move forward according to His will.

REVIVE, REFRESH, RENEW

Reflect/Journal

Day 28
I THINK I'M ON TO SOMETHING

Have you ever been in a place where you may say to yourself, "I think I have this now!" You may have been confused about one thing, and then all of a sudden, out of the blue, you receive the clarity that you've been praying about for a long time. And then, you may find yourself trying to connect the dots of life. You may say to yourself, "Finally, in this particular area of reasoning, I got it."

Think of that one area that you have been praying about for a long time, and you finally received a breakthrough. And I also want you to think of another area where you haven't quite received it, but you're almost there.

Life is a journey— a wonderful journey— full of surprises, but all the things that we face in life teach us a valuable lesson. We are in the class of life, daily learning something that will make us better for tomorrow. You are about to embark on a journey with the Lord that you have never been on before. Buckle your seat belts, and get ready for something new, refreshing, and unexpected. We are taking the limits off of your life— off of God.

Allow Him to show you what He has invested in you—this treasure that is in you, that will bring value to your life. God wants you to know today that you are valuable. His investment in you is priceless, and nothing can stop what He is about to do. Look for vision and understanding in this season— information released to take you further beyond where you are now or could have ever imagined.

> *But we have this treasure in earthen vessels, that the excellency of the power may be of God, and not of us.*
>
> — 2 CORINTHIANS 4:7

> *Father God, we know that it is in You that we move, breathe, and have our being in and that without You, we will be lost. So we thank You, Father, that we find refuge and strength in You. We thank You, for Your strength is made perfect in our weakness, and as we present this area to You today, we are praying that You will supernaturally give us divine direction as to how to move forward in this place and show us what valuable lesson we should learn while we are here. In Jesus' Name. Amen.*

> *And he said unto me, My grace is sufficient for thee: for my strength is made perfect in weakness. Most gladly therefore will I rather glory in my infirmities, that the power of Christ may rest upon me.*
>
> — 2 CORINTHIANS 12:9

* * *

Take a moment to think, reflect, pray, and meditate. As you are praying, God will begin to highlight what to write regarding what's needed in your life to move forward according to His will.

Reflect/Journal

Day 29
OPEN MY EYES

Living without God is like being blindfolded and feeling your way through everything. And the ironic thing about this is that you don't know that you are blind until your eyes are opened. We may find ourselves feeling our way through life, making decisions, while not entirely sure that they are the right ones. However, we try to do our best based on what we know. It was not until my spiritual senses were awakened by God's love that I realized this. He wants us to see our current state so we can realize that we need help through life.

God holds the key to all of what our future entails. What we watch either feeds His plan or ours; what we listen to will grow His plan or ours. What will we believe? Will we cultivate His plan or ours? It's either our flesh or our spirit. Our flesh will continue to war with our spirit. So if we starve and kill the flesh daily, then the spirit of God will be in control.

Moments of uncertainty will come, but may the strong man win. The battle is already won because the Lord is strong in battle. He will walk through the battle with us, and the Word is your shield for He is the living Word. The Word is our map in battle, the lamp unto our feet, and the light unto our path (Psalm 119:105). It illuminates the right path and timing of every move, as the Holy Spirit gauges every action.

The Holy Spirit will keep our minds and motives in order. Our body can be in chaos without the peace of God, and the war within will make you lose the war without. Don't move from the place of grace, the space that God has given you to flow. You have the ability because He is working through you; it is only in Him that we can produce what is inside of us. We can't receive the information and then leave the table and try to do it on our own without His instruction. We have to stay with Him and follow it through. Commit to the process!

> *If you love me, keep my commands. And I will ask the Father, and he will give you another advocate to help you and be with you forever—the Spirit of truth. The world cannot accept him, because it neither sees him nor knows him. But you know him, for he lives with you and will be in you.*
>
> — JOHN 14:15–17

> *And he has identified us as his own by placing the Holy Spirit in our hearts as the first installment that guarantees everything he has promised us.*
>
> — 2 CORINTHIANS 1:22

> *Father God, in the Name of Jesus, my prayer today is that my eyes be opened and that I am enlightened by Your truth that I was not aware of yesterday. I know that it is through communion and Your Word that I am able to learn more of You as well as more of who You desire for me to be. Psalm 119:18 says, "Father, Open my eyes, that I may behold wondrous things out of your law." In the precious Name of Jesus. Amen.*

> *Father, open the eyes of my hearts enlighten or so that I may know what is the hope to which you called me, what are the riches of his glorious inheritance in the saints.*
>
> — EPHESIANS 1:18

For you were formerly darkness, but now you are Light in the Lord; walk as children of Light.

— EPHESIANS 5:8

But you are a chosen race, a royal priesthood, a holy nation, a people for God's own possession, so that you may proclaim the excellencies of Him who has called you out of darkness into His marvelous light.

— 1 PETER 2:9

* * *

Take a moment to think, reflect, pray, and meditate. As you are praying, God will begin to highlight what to write regarding what's needed in your life to move forward according to His will.

Reflect/Journal

Day 30
CHARGED AND READY

Many of us around the world have tapped into technology with cell phones, iPads, laptops, and much more. So, let's talk about the cell phone. Many of us have one, and most of us don't leave home without it. Before going on a long trip or even a quick run to the grocery store, we want to make sure we have our phones. In our homes, there are plenty of electronic sources to charge our devices. We make sure we have our cord chargers and our electronic sources for backup, just in case the battery runs low or loses complete power.

What happens when you forget your charger, and you're out with no way to charge your phone? What if someone is trying to contact you or if there's an emergency? What will you do? Will you wait until you get home or around someone else with a power source to charge your device?

As Believers, we have to be stored up with enough spiritual ammunition and know where our divine source is when we are running low. We have those seasons in our lives where we may feel 100 percent, invincible, and like nothing can stop us. Then, we may have those times where we are praying to God, "Where are You? I don't feel you. I feel disconnected."

Unlike electrical sources, when we are fully charged, we unplug them. But as born-again Christians, we have to always stay plugged in to our divine source. We have to eat our daily bread every day, and we have to talk to our Father every day and commune with Him. Even in those times when we don't feel like He's there, we still have to stay connected.

Well, when we're running on E, and we are worn out from life's issues and circumstances, we can always plug back in and get charged—charged and ready for anything that life brings. We don't know what will happen every day of our lives, but we have the Word of God that is written on the tablets of our heart. So, no matter what comes along our path, we have the tools and wisdom to be able to sustain us in the midst of anything we face.

> *Father God, in the Name of Jesus, I thank You today for being my divine source. You are my shepherd, my covering, and You have everything that I need. I know that it is in the Word of God where I find strength and encouragement to take me through and sustain me in every trial that I face. I want to live a life charged and ready to face anything that comes on a day-to-day basis. I pray to You, Father, that I will always be equipped with the armor of God. Even in those unexpected situations, I will know how to grab the sword of the spirit, which is the Word of God, and use it in my time of need. In Jesus' Name. Amen.*

> *Put on the full armor of God, so that you can take your stand against the devil's schemes. For our struggle is not against flesh and blood, but against the rulers, against the authorities, against the powers of this dark world and against the spiritual forces of evil in the heavenly realms. Therefore put on the full armor of God, so that when the day of evil comes, you may be able to stand your ground, and after you have done everything, to stand. Stand firm then, with the belt of truth buckled around your waist, with the breastplate of righteousness in place, and with your feet fitted with the readiness that comes from the gospel of peace.*

In addition to all this, take up the shield of faith, with which you can extinguish all the flaming arrows of the evil one. Take the helmet of salvation and the sword of the Spirit, which is the word of God.

— EPHESIANS 6:11–17

* * *

Take a moment to think, reflect, pray, and meditate. As you are praying, God will begin to highlight what to write regarding what's needed in your life to move forward according to His will.

Reflect/Journal

Bonus: Day 31
WORSHIP IGNITED

Always remember that God wants your undivided attention. When you're in a relationship, and you rely too much on the other person to provide what only God can, a separation is coming. He's a jealous God. Man is not able to give us what God can give. It becomes a form of worship when we begin to totally rely on a source other than God. Of course, God will use others to bless you in your life, whether in words or in deeds. That's what we are here for, to be helpers to one another, but not in the form of worship! We bless God, not the vessel He uses to bless us.

Sometimes it's difficult to do this. Well, aren't we supposed to show our love and show that we appreciate the other person for what they do? Yes, we are, but where is your heart concerning the matter? Okay, so I know you're asking, "How can I properly give the Lord what's due to Him while still appreciate my spouse, friend, or future mate?"

Well, the big question is, do you have a consistent prayer life? And is your time in studying the Word of God consistent, as well?

Being washed in the Word and seeking the Lord daily will strengthen your spirit. It'll help you see how to properly distribute what you pour out. There are no good things in the flesh, and we were created to worship. We should not rely on someone else because man does not have the capability to give us what only our Father can. We will overwork someone because of our expectations of them.

It's all about putting things into perspective. If there is a place in your life (heart) where you have been abandoned, rejected, or neglected, you may not properly discern in this area where you may still be hurting. The human nature is that an action requires a response, as in correlation with a reflex. You, sometimes without reason, respond to matters because of what's deep inside of you without realizing it. And sometimes, this occurs so that we can properly deal with certain matters.

> *Father God, today I present my body to You as a living sacrifice. I present my gifts and God-given abilities to You so that all can be used for Your glory. My prayer today is that my life be an act of worship to You. I pray that everything about my inner being glorifies You. You deserve the sacrifice of my life because You gave me life. It belongs to You. Let my hands be used to impart and create. Let my mouth encourage and uplift. Let my feet carry Your peace and the Good News everywhere I go, as I know that You are with me. I pray that as I open my mouth, that You speak, uproot, rebuild, and establish in Jesus' name. Fill me up, even more with Your spirit, so that You may be glorified only through my life in Jesus' Name. Amen.*

* * *

Take a moment to think, reflect, pray, and meditate. As you are praying, God will begin to highlight what to write regarding what's needed in your life to move forward according to His will.

REVIVE, REFRESH, RENEW

Reflect/Journal

Bonus: Day 32
IDENTITY RECOVERED

Allow me to remind you of who God created you to be. God has spoken over you and created you before time began, so that you can walk out life in your full identity. Your identity was stolen by lies, religion, sin, etc. But the thief of your identity has been caught. Now, protect what God has revealed, and conceal it in your heart.

God is in your heart. Put a bolt lock on it, so God will be the only one with the key. The devil stole your identity, but God has restored it because you allowed Him to search your heart. He saw some things while you were off-guard.

You are protected. Angels are at the door of your heart and your garden to stop anything or anyone unauthorized to come in. Love is authorized. God is authorized. The peace of God is authorized. A total surrender to God is authorized. Allow Him to invade your heart, captivate your mind, and restore your soul.

We have magnified and given too much power to the things of this world, making these things idols and giving them more glory than God. Let's acknowledge God and put to death everything that we have put before Him. We have to make a choice. We have worshipped the god of this world and whatever it brings for far too long. God has been sitting on the throne, waiting for us to get tired of the inevitable.

God is long-suffering, but now it's time for us to change. We can't lose any more ground. We have lost our momentum, and we have to get it back. Don't worry or focus on how long you have been out of momentum, just get back in the game. May the best man win! And if you stick with God, just know that the battle is already won.

> *Your eyes saw my unformed body; all the days ordained for me were written in your book before one of them came to be.*
>
> *— PSALM 139:16*

> *Father, in the Name of Jesus, I draw nigh to You today. I seek to know You more, Lord. Show me Your face, so that I may know who I am and who You have created me to be. I will no longer try to live life on my own, making decisions based on my emotions. Fill me with Your Holy Spirit. Fill me up so that I no longer see me, but You only. You alone are the only One who can save me from myself. It's in You that I know who I am and who You desire for me to be. In the mighty Name of Jesus. Amen.*

* * *

Take a moment to think, reflect, pray, and meditate. As you are praying, God will begin to highlight what to write regarding what's needed in your life to move forward according to His will.

REVIVE, REFRESH, RENEW

Reflect/Journal

Affirmations

- I am an **entrepreneur**.
- I am **debt-free.**
- I am **emotionally stable.**
- I am **no longer a victim.**
- I am **victorious.**
- I will **accomplish my goals.**
- I'm **not a failure.**
- I'm a **winner.**
- I'm **healed.**
- I'm a **survivor.**
- I am **made whole.**
- I have a **renewed mind.**
- I'm **more than a conqueror.**
- I will **not give into temptation.**
- I **can do all things through Christ** who strengthens me.
- I **will not settle for less** than I deserve.
- I **deserve the best.**
- The **best is yet to come.**
- It's time for me to **move forward.**
- Today is a **new start.**
- This is my **fresh start.**
- There are **no more boundaries**; the limits are off.

AFFIRMATIONS

- I embrace **total happiness.**
- I'm **allergic to negativity.**
- I **partner with destiny.**
- I'm **rewriting my book**, and it has a happy ending.
- This **journey is fulfilling.**
- I will **make the best out of something negative.**
- I will **learn from my errors and grow.**
- My **issues don't define me.**
- My past has **no control over what's next.**
- I am **unified with promise.**

Promises of God

THE PROMISES OF GOD'S GOODNESS

When things get tough, it can be easy to focus on ourselves and our difficulties. Read these Bible promises about who God is, and let them lift your eyes away from your own situation to the God who is infinitely good.

- *Psalm 145:9* - The Lord is good to all; He has compassion on all he has made.

- *1 Chronicles 16:34* - Give thanks to the Lord, for He is good; His love endures forever.

- Psalm 100:5 - For the Lord is good and His love endures forever; His faithfulness continues through all generations.

- *James 1:17* - Every good and perfect gift is from above, coming down from the Father of the heavenly lights, who does not change like shifting shadows.

- *2 Samuel 7:28* - Sovereign Lord, You are God! Your covenant is trustworthy, and You have promised these good things to your servant.

- *Psalm 19:7* The law of the Lord is perfect, refreshing the soul. The statutes of the Lord are trustworthy, making wise the simple.

- *Psalm 34:8* - Taste and see that the Lord is good; blessed is the one who takes refuge in Him.

- *Nahum 1:7* - The Lord is good, a refuge in times of trouble. He cares for those who trust in Him.

- *Psalm 84:11* - For the Lord God is a sun and shield; the Lord bestows favour and honour; no good thing does He withhold from those whose walk is blameless.

THE PROMISES OF GOD'S FAITHFULNESS

Hold on to these promises that God is with you in your individual situation. Remember the time in the Bible when God gave Noah a rainbow as a sign that God keeps His promises. As He was faithful to Noah, He will be faithful to you.

- *Isaiah 40:29* - He gives strength to the weary and increases the power of the weak.

- *Isaiah 40:31* - But those who hope in the LORD will renew their strength. They will soar on wings like eagles; they will run and not grow weary, they will walk and not be faint.

- *Isaiah 43:2* - When you pass through the waters, I will be with you; and when you pass through the rivers, they will not sweep over you. When you walk through the fire, you will not be burned; the flames will not set you ablaze.

- *Jeremiah 29:11* - For I know the plans I have for you," declares the LORD, "plans to prosper you and not to harm you, plans to give you hope and a future.

- *Deuteronomy 31:8* - The LORD himself goes before you and will be with you; He will never leave you nor forsake you. Do not be afraid; do not be discouraged.

- *Joshua 1:9* - Have I not commanded you? Be strong and courageous. Do not be afraid; do not be discouraged, for the Lord your God will be with you wherever you go.

- *Psalm 23:4* - Even though I walk through the darkest valley, I will fear no evil, for You are with me; Your rod and Your staff, they comfort me.

- *Philippians 4:6–7* - Do not be anxious about anything, but in every situation, by prayer and petition, with thanksgiving, present your requests to God. And the peace of God, which transcends all understanding, will guard your hearts and your minds in Christ Jesus.

THE PROMISES OF GOD'S PROVISION

The Bible is full of examples of God providing for His people. Time and again, the God of life promises to provide, whether our need is land, food, shelter, comfort, or hope.

- *Matthew 6:31–33* - So do not worry, saying, "What shall we eat?" or "What shall we drink?" or "What shall we wear?" For the pagans run after all these things, and your heavenly Father knows that you need them. But seek first His kingdom and His righteousness, and all these things will be given to you, as well.

- *Proverbs 3:5–6* - Trust in the Lord with all your heart and lean not on your own understanding; in all your ways submit to Him, and He will make your paths straight.

THE PROMISES OF GOD THROUGH JESUS

During His time on earth, Jesus made many promises about the peace and hope He offers us. This collection of Jesus' promises gives us great hope and reminds us that He truly is the Savior of the world.

- *Matthew 11:28–30* - Come to me, all you who are weary and burdened, and I will give you rest. Take My yoke upon you and learn from Me, for I am gentle and humble in heart, and you will find rest for your souls. For My yoke is easy and My burden is light.

- *John 14:6* - Jesus answered, "I am the way and the truth and the life. No one comes to the Father except through me."

- *John 8:12* - I am the light of the world. Whoever follows me will never walk in darkness, but will have the light of life.

- *Isaiah 61:1* - The Spirit of the Sovereign Lord is on me, because the Lord has anointed me to proclaim good news to the poor. He has sent me to bind up the brokenhearted, to proclaim freedom for the captives and release from darkness for the prisoners.

- *John 14:15–16* - If you love Me, keep My commands. And I will ask the Father, and He will give you another advocate to help you and be with you forever.

- *John 10:10* The thief comes only to steal and kill and destroy; I have come that they may have life, and have it to the full.

THE PROMISES OF GOD REGARDING PRAYER

Prayer is so powerful! Reflect on these Bible verses about prayer, and let God's promises spur you on to pray to your Heavenly Father. Share your hopes and needs with Him, today.

- *James 1:5* - If any of you lacks wisdom, you should ask God, who gives generously to all without finding fault, and it will be given to you.

- *Mark 11:24* - Therefore I tell you, whatever you ask for in prayer, believe that you have received it, and it will be yours.

- *Psalm 37:4* - Take delight in the Lord, and He will give you the desires of your heart.

- *John 14:13* - And I will do whatever you ask in My Name, so that the Father may be glorified in the Son. You may ask Me for anything in My Name, and I will do it.

- *Luke 11:9–13* - So I say to you: Ask and it will be given to you; seek and you will find; knock and the door will be opened to you. For everyone who asks receives; the one who seeks finds; and to the one who knocks, the door will be opened. Which of you fathers, if your son asks for a fish, will give him a snake instead? Or, if he asks for an egg, will give him a scorpion? If you then, though you are evil, know how to give good gifts to your children, how much more will your Father in heaven give the Holy Spirit to those who ask Him!

THE PROMISES OF GOD REGARDING SALVATION

Finally, take a moment to remember the most precious of all— God's promises to us! Thanks to Jesus' sacrifice on the Cross, God promises to forgive us and give us eternal life with Him.

- *John 3:16* - For God so loved the world that He gave His one and only Son, that whoever believes in Him shall not perish but have eternal life.

- *1 John 1:9* - If we confess our sins, He is faithful and just and will forgive us our sins and purify us from all unrighteousness.

- *2 Chronicles 7:14* - If My people, who are called by My name, will humble themselves and pray and seek My face and turn from their wicked ways, then I will hear from heaven, and I will forgive their sin and will heal their land.

- *John 8:36* - So if the Son sets you free, you will be free indeed.

- *Romans 10:9–10* - If you declare with your mouth, "Jesus is Lord," and believe in your heart that God raised Him from the dead, you will be saved. For it is with your heart that you believe and are justified, and it is with your mouth that you profess your faith and are saved.

Daily Prayer

Father God, in the Name of Jesus, we thank You for every day that we arise. We rise with purpose and power, ready to begin our day. Each day has a purpose. But this is the day that You have made, and we shall rejoice and be glad in it. Today, I accept the command to rise and shine my light so that men may see the glory of You, Father. My prayer today is that they see Your good works, receive Your love, and glorify You. For Your kingdom come and Your Will be done on Earth, as it is in heaven. I humble myself under Your mighty Hand to be a vessel used to perform the task that is set before me, today.

Father God, I die to my flesh today, repenting of any old habits that do not bring You glory. And today, I am renewed to follow the sinless example of Jesus Christ, my Savior. I lay aside every weight and the sin that tries to grip me in my most vulnerable state. For Your strength is made perfect in my weakness. I lay every care at Your feet, and I trade in my sorrow for Your love, joy, and peace. The peace of God surpasses all understanding.

I dress myself in the full armor of God. I cover my head with the Helmet of Salvation. I cover my chest with the Breastplate of Righteousness. I arm myself with the Sword of the Spirit. I am protected by the Shield of Faith, girded up with the Belt of Truth, and my feet are anointed by the Gospel of Peace. So, today I die to my fleshly desires, so that You can live through me. For You are my daily bread, and I wash myself in the Word. The Word of God is a lamp to my feet and a light to my path.

Even when I walk through the Valley of the Shadow of Death, I will fear no evil, for I know You are with me. Today, we are seated far above principalities and power, for You have given us the authority to trample on scorpions and serpents. We have power over the enemy, and nothing will harm us.

We thank You, Father, for You have disarmed the principalities and powers. We declare every dead branch in our lives be cut off, and we destroy every oath and vow made secretly against us. We know that no weapon formed against us shall prosper. When the enemy comes in like a flood, we thank You for lifting up a standard against him. When we resist the devil, he will flee seven ways, because we have victory over the enemy in every area our lives. We thank You, Father, for being our Sword and Shield, the Giver of grace and glory. Help us to walk uprightly before You. For You will not withhold any good thing from us.

We love You, Lord, for You are our strength. We cry, "Holy! Holy! Holy! You are the Lord of hosts! The whole earth is full of Your glory!" We exalt You, Lord, and worship at Your footstool. We fear and give reverence to You, Father. We stand in awe of You. By Your abundant lovingkindness, we enter Your house. At Your holy temple, we bow in reverence for You, Lord. You don't require much of us— just to reverence You, walk in Your ways, and to love You with our whole heart and soul.

I humble myself under the mighty Name of Jesus, and I declare victory over every area of my life and my family. Every situation and trial that may seem to be exaggerated by the devil is made null and void, and destroyed in the Name of Jesus.

Lord, we thank You for the victory in the areas of the mind, body, and soul. We yield all areas of weakness, for Your strength is made perfect in all of them. I pray for exhilaration in my relationship with God, finances, marriage, relationships, ministry, completion of tasks, and business ventures— that all will manifest in the mighty name of Jesus.

I pray that every demonic distraction will cease, and as I resist the devil, he will flee. So, Father, I walk in the authority of the power of God that resides inside of me. I pray that as I am walking in obedience to Your will, that new levels of power be released to overcome any trial, accomplish any task, and complete every ministry assignment. Nothing will cause me to back down because the power of God is the governing factor for forward progression in the Name of Jesus Christ. Amen.

Final Message

I want to encourage you to not give up on your life, purpose, dreams, or visions. But most importantly, do not give up on God. He loves you, and there is a plan for your life. I know, sometimes things that happen in your life may be totally discouraging, and it may seem as if you may never recover, but *you will*. If you are reading this final message of this thirty day devotional, this is specifically for you.

The devil comes to kill, steal, and destroy, but Jesus came so that you may have life *more abundantly. Your life should be more than average.* Don't settle for anything less than God's best for you! You have great value. Don't believe any lies that were told to you by anyone— even yourself — about your future. God had a plan in mind when He created you. You are were carefully crafted by the only True and Living God, Creator of all things.

There are so many people waiting to hear your story of overcoming all that you endured, from childbirth up until now. Everyone has a story to tell, and yours matters. too. Don't hesitate; don't wait any longer. You will overcome by your testimony. Expose what has been holding you captive for so long. Let the secrets out; pull the rug up! Now, it's time to deal with what has been haunting you for so long. Unlock the jail of your heart, and release the hurt, pain, and regrets of the past. It's time to *live*!

Don't you want to live?! I know that may seem difficult to grasp at

FINAL MESSAGE

the moment, but you can do it. You can do all things through Christ that strengthens you. If you feel like you don't have the strength to do it on your own, that's okay. God has people around you, rooting for you. Do you know that you have your own cheering section?

It's time for an extreme makeover. Moving forward, your life will never look the same. You will look at your past and smile, instead of cry. Replace thankfulness for sorrow, because it made you who you are today. Always remember that you are not what you have experienced; your experiences do not dictate your future. What's ahead is far greater than your past and your now. You may not feel it or believe it right now, but while you're reading this, your faith is growing and expanding.

Faith comes by hearing the Word of God. The Word comes to reveal, heal, remove, impart, cut away, add to, multiply, and divide. Trade in all of your heavy burdens for the joy of the Lord. You can rejoice when things are going well, because with God, you will always have a good outcome; it's guaranteed every time. Do you believe? Just believe, trust, hope, and live again. And for those of you who don't feel like you have ever really lived your life, well, you are in for a great surprise! With God, you will embark upon a great adventure with so many unexpected surprises that you wouldn't even imagine.

Walk in it! It's your time!

About the Author

Crystal Love, a native of Baltimore, Maryland, is a wife, mother, servant, and prophet in the Body of Christ. She is a certified Christian counselor, licensed cosmetologist, and certified Holistic Nutritionist who walks boldly in her purpose. She utilizes her academic background and experience to assist and push others to *find* out their purpose, *focus* on it, and *accomplish* it! Under the umbrella of her organization, Vision Advancement, she helps her clients navigate the process from start to finish.

In 2011, God gave her a vision entitled Holistic Ministries. This ministry was birthed out of a season of pain. During this time, she grieved her father's death, while trying to establish herself as a single mother. At that stage in her life, she recognized the correlation between her overall wellness and spiritual health.

These three Scriptures had a significant impact on Crystal:

- "When Jesus saw him lying there and learned that he had been in this condition for a long time, he asked him, "Do you want to get well?" — *John 5:6*
- "Beloved, I wish above all things that thou mayest prosper and be in health, even as thy soul prospereth." — *3 John 2:2*
- "The thief cometh not, but for to steal, and to kill, and to destroy: I am come that they might have life and that they might have it more abundantly." — *John 10:10*

Upon meditating on these Scriptures, the depth of God's love was revealed to her. She recognized the impact of one's total wellness, as a grounded life glorifies God! From that moment forward, she approached wellness from a holistic standpoint, understanding the significance of balance, consistency, and discipline within every aspect of a person's life.

And to this day, Crystal Love is dedicated to serving people abroad. She has a deep, heartfelt passion for seeing others become healed and delivered spiritually, emotionally, socially, and physically.

> Beloved, I pray that in all aspects, you may prosper and be in good health, just as your soul prospers.
>
> — 3 JOHN 1:2

For more books and updates:
www.crystallove-theauthor.com

 facebook.com/crystal_love

 twitter.com/crystalcauthor

 instagram.com/holisticministriesclove

www.ingramcontent.com/pod-product-compliance
Lightning Source LLC
Chambersburg PA
CBHW072156070526
44585CB00015B/1164